MW00612581

Management for Professionals

For further volumes:
http://www.springer.com/series/10101

Argang Ghadiri • Andreas Habermacher •
Theo Peters

Neuroleadership

A Journey Through the Brain
for Business Leaders

 Springer

Argang Ghadiri
Theo Peters
Business Administration
Bonn-Rhine-Sieg
University of Applied Sciences
Sankt Augustin
Germany

Andreas Habermacher
ctp, corporate training programmes
Zuerich
Switzerland

Revised and adapted translation of the book Neuroleadership, published in German by Gabler Verlag, Wiesbaden in 2011.

ISSN 2192-8096   ISSN 2192-810X (electronic)
ISBN 978-3-642-30164-3   ISBN 978-3-642-30165-0 (eBook)
DOI 10.1007/978-3-642-30165-0
Springer Heidelberg New York Dordrecht London

Library of Congress Control Number: 2012950142

Printed on acid-free paper

Springer is part of Springer Science+Business Media (www.springer.com)

Preface

The brain is a massive network of connections and the journey to this book also started in the electronic web of connections and interactions—the Internet. Each of us had developed a passion for neuroscience and its impact in business in different locations. Professor Theo Peters and Argang Ghadiri had worked together on the German version of this book and they first interacted with Andy Habermacher on an online neuroleadership forum. They had been deeply impressed with the papers and writings of Andy. Andy had separately developed his passion after being introduced to neuroscience by Dr. Srinivasan Pillay during a course in New York focused on executive coaching. This online interaction led to some personal discussion on how we could collaborate closer and in what form. From this sprung forth the concept of this book. This shows more than anything the power of the network and of networks in general, whether they be social, electronic or in the brain itself.

This book is grounded in the German version and yet it is also different. We have worked through it and turned it into an enriched English version – some concepts have been added to, some more depth has been added. What you read here is the result of a strong collaboration. It is the fruit of our efforts and it has blossomed into what we feel is something that can give you value and powerful insights into the brain and leadership. More than anything else we hope that these concepts will not stay in the book but will be taken and implemented concretely in the workplace.

In our collaboration we have also had to practice what we preach over the following pages and our collaboration has proven to be engaging, exciting, challenging and fun all at the same time. We have worked hard but enjoyed it immensely. We have discussed ideas and also thrown out ideas but all understanding the final goal we wanted to achieve. We have positively criticised and given each other compliments where and when necessary. In short it has been hard work but very much fun at the same time.

Indeed, any book a major product and requires commitment and hard work. A book also is, in some respects, the product of the people who have helped to develop us, the authors. It is the synthesis of ideas and thoughts and the knowledge we have collected over the years, and many, many people have been involved in this process. There have been people who have helped us directly and indirectly— we have drawn from other authors, researchers, academics and scientists. We have discussed amongst ourselves, with colleagues, on online forums and through our formal work. Many of the ideas can be traced to individuals but much cannot be.

And this is why we would in general like to thank all the people who we have interacted with over the years and whose input has helped us to develop our own ideas. The number of people is too large to mention specific names here. We also believe the wealth of this knowledge lies in the mix and not the quantity—it is the right mix of ingredients in the kitchen that create a wonderful, tasty dish and not just the individual ingredients.

Importantly though, this would not have been possible without the help of our publisher, and our specific thanks therefore go to Springer, and especially Barbara Fess, who so quickly realised that this was a book they wanted to publish. We reached a formal agreement very quickly and this made the publishing process painless.

We now only need to express our wish that you enjoy the book and are able to draw out some of the knowledge to enrich your life and your experience of being a leader. We hope this book proves as useful to you as it has already proven to be to each of us.

Argang Ghadiri
Andy Habermacher
Theo Peters

Contents

List of Figures

List of Tables

About the Authors

Argang Ghadiri completed his studies of Business Administration in the master's programme of the Mercator School of Management (University of Duisburg-Essen, Germany) and the Aalto School of Economics (Aalto University, Finland) and gained his Bachelor degree at the Bonn-Rhine-Sieg University of Applied Sciences (Germany) and FHS St.Gallen University of Applied Sciences (Switzerland). In addition to his scientific work as a tutor and scientific assistant he gained practical experience in consulting and auditing firms. He is currently collaborating with Professor Theo Peters as research associate at the department of Business Administration in Sankt Augustin.

argang.ghadiri@h-brs.de

Andy Habermacher started his career in linguistics and language training before founding his own company focusing on communication and soft skills to executives. He qualified as a Certified Master Coach in 2008 and followed this with studies on neuroscience as applied to coaching through Dr. Srinivasan Pillay and the NeuroBusiness Group. His business now focuses on neuroscience applications for business and leadership development. In 2011 he published "The Fox Factor" which takes us into the unconscious processes of how we are influenced by status and personality.

andy@leading-brains.com

Prof. Dr. Theo Peters studied Business Administration at the Rheinisch-Westfälische University in Aachen (Germany) and subsequently Economics at the University of Cologne where he also completed his doctoral studies. Before taking on his position at Bonn-Rhine-Sieg University of Applied Sciences he worked as a business consultant in organisational and personnel development. In addition to his lecturing and research activities at numerous universities Professor Theo Peters gives seminars and presentations on current business administration themes.

theo.peters@h-brs.de

Introduction

Though the field of neuroleadership is yet to break into mainstream business theory, it is not new. The term itself was coined in 2006 by David Rock and there has been an ever-increasing flow of books on the brain in many contexts including leadership, marketing and management. You may therefore ask why write another book on the brain and leadership. The answer to this is simple and highlights the approach we have taken here. There is no book that takes the uninitiated through the whole journey of neuroleadership. This book describes the background of the neurosciences, outlines the technology, explains the brain, introduces protagonists and defines how it can be applied to business.

This book will therefore give you all the basic background information you will need to become a neuroleader. As we keep noting, there is a mass of information in the market and our goals is not to go into the specific details but to provide you with enough information to get a much clearer idea of the brain and how it functions, specifically in application to business.

Our work has also asked us to question time and time again what neuroleadership is and what the brain is and how this influences our thinking and actions. This led us to the work of Klaus Grawe where we found a fundamental description of the neuroscientific basis of human beings and their interactions with the environment. If we look into the brain we must go to its base functioning—the functioning that defines us as human beings—and then work upwards and outwards. We realised that many books had focused on the outer layers, so to speak, but none had gone to the fundamental level of human interactions—the basic needs and desires that drive each of us. This is what is the second big difference in this book. We go into the basic needs of human beings and from this develop and look at organisational and personnel development and various leadership concepts. The third big difference is very few books have given clear organisational and leadership applications, methodologies that can be applied across broad levels of the workforce but have focused on, interesting all the same, some specific interactions and manifestations of the brain in the workplace. We aim here to give a concrete methodology that you can implement in the workplace.

To summarise, this book then aims to

– Give a complete overview of neuroleadership, from neuroscience, basic functioning of the brain, human basic needs and applications in the workplace

– Highlight the importance of human basic needs in the workplace for daily interactions and motivational goals
– Give a model that can be applied in the workplace and a tool for leaders to implement to be able to make the workplace more brain friendly and hence tap into the full potential of their workers

We start the journey in Chap. 1 by first looking at the definition of neuroleadership and the development of "neuro" business terms. Here we also take an historical view of the concept of man from homo economicus to the brain-directed man. This gives us concepts on which much of the economic theory is based—all models rely on a model of the human interacting within it and this model will influence the characteristics of the model.

We then move in Chap. 2 into the brain itself. We look at the development, the chemical interactions, the regional functions and some of the history and interesting insights from neuroscience. We touch on the technology so that we can understand what this actually does and how brain activity is measured, but we also look at emotions and the functional and physical representations of emotional activity.

Chapter 3 now moves onto the key protagonists in the field of neuroscience in business contexts. This helps to give us an understanding of where we stand in the literature and some of the key influential figures that have helped to form the concept of neuroleadership so far.

Chapter 4 moves into what we can consider the heart of the book. Here we look into the work of Klaus Grawe and our basic human needs. We will take you through the neuroscientific basis of the basic needs, and these are grounded in all human personality—indeed they are the result of over 100 years of work into human personality and psychology and therapy. The basic needs are important, not just because of their representation in human beings, but because these will be directly linked to our motivational drives: our urges, our drives, our impetus to fulfil or protect our basic needs or the imbalance of these. This is the manifestation of brain biology and its interactions and the subsequent representation into human social contexts.

In Chap. 5 we take these neuroscientifically based basic needs and transpose them onto organisational and personnel development tools and leadership concepts. This is where we take a fundamental look at business science and combine this with neuroscientific insights, looking at whether these tools through the spectacles of neuroscience and the basic needs will give us the answers to their effectiveness. Their effectiveness, because each tool will target and activate different regions and needs in the brain and hence have different impacts on different people and groups of people. The reasons lie in the neural representation of these tools and the neural impact on the workspace which will depend directly on a person's basic needs, their fulfilment and their own personal motivational goals which we discuss in Chap. 4. We aim in this chapter to highlight some standard tools and concepts but do not aim to create a new "neuro" technique. We also only focus on a selection of tools, for the sake of simplicity and to demonstrate the thought process.

From this analysis of tools and concepts in organisational development and leadership we then move to a model for the concrete implementation of this in corporations. The ACTIVE model we propose, in Chap. 6, is a methodology that can be implemented in corporations to assess the basic needs of employees and hence gain insights to these and moreover to gain insights into the motivational schemata. From this the neuroleader will be able to then make changes to the environment in organisational and leadership styles to best tap into the personal profile of the employee and of groups of employees. This will therefore look into the very core of the human being and hence enable this particular person to, from a brain-based perspective, tap into their full personal potential.

We can only access a person's full potential if the biology of the brain is aligned with the psychological perspective of the world. If we can do this, any given person will be able to fulfil the maximum potential and furthermore grow and continue learning and improving—learning, we note in numerous places, we know from brain science is always possible. The environment must fit and the motivational goals must be aligned, however.

This is where we end this particular journey into the brain. Further publications we are currently working on will answer some specific questions you may ask: the PERFECT model we will expand in future work in addition to some of the situational impacts on the brain and relevance for leadership, e.g. of crises interventions, creativity and team learning.

We include a learning check which we encourage you to use to make sure you have extracted the maximum possible from this book. This particular journey into neuroleadership will then be complete.

Neuroleadership: The Backdrop

1

This chapter aims to answer the simple question of what neuroleadership is. In addition we need to understand where it ties into current economic theory, if at all, and where it ties into the field of business and management theory, if at all. We will therefore outline what the current and developing "neuro" fields are, where they overlap, and where they tie together. We also propose a new term to create consistency within the fields of research. This will be followed by an historical overview of man's concept of man—the being that economic and business theory is based upon. This will lead us to the stage we are at today in defining neuroleadership and also that of defining the concept of man according to the brain.

Objectives

- Understand how neuroleadership ties into current economic and management theory
- Understand the historical development of man's concept of man leading to the most current view of the brain-directed man

1.1 Introduction

Fields of economic endeavour and management theory are not planned processes. There is no central administration for the planning of economic theory, management theory or business theory. These processes follow an organic development which sprout out of new ideas and insights and from these new concepts are developed and early adopters will charge into the market place. This charge may gain momentum or it may lose steam and fade away to be replaced by another concept, another theory, and another basis for understanding economics at the micro or macro level. Some of these ideas do take root and they grow and develop and are taken on by a larger and larger community of protagonists and experts. The newspapers will follow, with a time lag, and so will academic journals and

A. Ghadiri et al., *Neuroleadership*, Management for Professionals,
DOI 10.1007/978-3-642-30165-0_1, © Springer-Verlag Berlin Heidelberg 2012

subsequently books will be published. Some of these books will be by lonesome rebels others will be by respected academics. And as these roots begin to spread we will then see the further developments of the tree, so to speak, starting to grow and become more substantial. This is indeed the case with all things "neuro" and business. Why do we say this? We do not say it because of the press but because of the massive amounts of research that are taking place in more and more fields. We can see cognitive neuroscience being combined with many fields and areas and we can see substantial investment into fields such as neuromarketing. But the more important sign is that universities have set up neuroeconomic departments and more are following suit. This is not just limited to universities but business schools are also taking this development very seriously. Economics Professors such as Ernst Fehr of Zurich University in Switzerland are researching and writing in the field of neuroeconomics in addition to "standard" economic theory.

As we write this in 2012, we see an acceleration of all things neuro—many are popular science applications and even pseudo-science but, for us, what is of crucial importance, is that there is massive increase in respected scientists and researchers moving in this field with an intensity and seriousness that will help define the future of neuroeconomics in a broader macro economic level and at the micro economic level of the business: looking into organisational and human interactions in doing business. This more serious take up started around 2005 and this chapter now aims to bring the terminology into line, to show you, the reader, what the developing fields are and to outline the historical perspective of man that will help us to understand where we are today and how this may influence economic thinking in the years to come. We have started at this point because we feel we need to understand the current fields before we go into the brain itself in Chap. 2.

1.2 Neuroeconomics

The addition of "neuro" to a term, sometimes seemingly at will, adds an element of science and an aura of authority and science to the "new" term. We here will describe the fields that we see are supported at a broader level in science, academia and in business. The term neuroeconomics is, for example, broadly supported in the academic community and is now firmly established as a part of economics, as we noted previously, with universities having departments of neuroeconomics. The word was first used formally in 2004 and came after a nearing of various disciplines and the new discipline was slowly forged together. 2005 saw the first formal meeting of the society of neuroscience presided over by Paul Glimcher, the first President of the Society (the idea for the society was first formulated by the key researchers in the field in 2003 and the first open meeting was held in 2004) (Glimcher et al. 2008). Neuroeconomics developed out of the realisation that, with the technologies now readily available, we can now look into that organ that defines human nature—the brain. From peering into those previously dark and invisible recesses of human nature we can now extract data, and pictures, that represent human behaviour. This can, many feel, lead to new and solidly founded insights into human behaviour. As economics is founded on human behaviour this can reform our view of economics and therefore the whole world of economic interactions. Neuroeconomics is the science of human behaviour in decision-making situations using the methodology and insights from neuroscience (see Camerer et al. 2004; Camerer et al. 2005; Glimcher et al. 2008). This field is currently booming for a number of reasons and specifically because the technology for peering into the brain have rapidly advanced and the technical sophistication of the machines has reached an astounding level in addition to the number of methods that are now available to scientists. This has enabled scientists and specifically neuroeconomists to look into brains and start to understand some of the processes involved in economic transactions in a clearer light—to be able to measure many of these processes and bring these to visual clarity through imaging technologies (see Sect. 2.6).

The classic description of homo economicus, that utility focused self-seeking utterly rational being, is therefore being reformed with solid scientific backing (see Sect. 1.5.1). One specific insight is that neuroscientists have also seen the importance of emotions (see Sect. 2.7) in controlling brain processes in more situations than previously considered: from buying products, to making financial decisions, to the interactions with each other at the workplace. Neuroscientists have indeed focused on these precise interactions and looked in more detail and with more clarity, than has ever before been possible, at what is happening in the brain during these interactions and decision making processes. Cognitive neuroscientists have focused on the interactions between different regions in the brain, and have mapped many of these regions into functional areas, and can understand now with some clarity as to how the brain is communicating within itself and what processes are controlling this.

This knowledge has also enabled neuroeconomists to understand what parts of the brain are influenced by decisions and what parts influence decisions and therefore has led to increasing research into this area. The field of neuroeconomics and neuroscience is, however, a multidisciplinary field involving neuroscientists, behavioural and applied psychologists and economists to name a few. To understand these interactions there are a wide range of disciplines that need to be involved. This is particularly important in neuroeconomics, as the focus is not on a "discrete" area such as chemical interactions between brain cells but rather on broader contexts involving a more complex interaction of human beings. In addition we can also see neuroeconomics in the light of microeconomic decision-making but also in the light of macro economic level of market movements across the economy. In addition further fields are also developing such as neurofinance and neuromanagement.

For the first step into neuroeconomics we will use a model put forward by Camerer et al. in 2005 (Camerer et al. 2005). This paper was specifically targeted at economists, tying economics into the brain and highlighting areas that economists need to focus on. This is a simplified model but gives a clearer understanding of brain processes and defines four types of brain information processing that influence our decisions. This in itself highlights that many of the processes in the brain are emotional and unconscious. This is an important realisation because much research and economic theory has focused only on

	Cognitive Processes	Affective Processes
Controlled Processes	I	II
Automatic Processes	III	IV

Fig. 1.1 The dimensions of neuronal functioning (From Camerer et al. 2005, p. 16)

conscious decisions which we now know to be only a part of the brain's neuronal functioning. These unconscious, automatic, process are of great interest to neuroeconomists and of great importance to us in neuroleadership also (Fig. 1.1):

- On the first axis we distinguish between affective and cognitive processes. Affective processes are those brain driven processes in relation to knowledge, memory and intention. Affective processes are those formed through emotions and drives. The key factor here is not the emotion but rather that they have affect i.e. a motivational factor, a drive. These can include emotions (joy, fear etc.), drives (thirst, hunger etc.) and motivational states (disgust, pain etc.).
- On the second axis we differentiate between controlled and automatic processes. Controlled processes are those that can be controlled and invoked deliberately by a person. They are deliberate, serial, effortful and, importantly, we have cognitive access to these. We can look at them with our mind and analyse them. On the other hand we have automatic processes which are driven below our level of consciousness. These are reflexive, often operate in parallel, are effortless and are not readily, if at all, accessible to our introspective cognitive processes. This is the much-popularised "unconscious".

This model highlights the various processes in the brain that many have ignored in economic theory and in the concepts of man that we will shortly look at. There has been an assumption that quadrant I—controlled and cognitive—have been the driving force of human thought and interactions. We can see from Camerer's, well-founded, model that we have generally ignored three aspects of the brain's processing. As we will discuss in Chap. 2 we now know that the underlying processes in III and IV but also in II can exert a huge influence on our interactions with the world. Indeed it is just these processes that are in the driving seat not those in I or as the psychologist Jonathan Haidt succinctly put it, "The emotional tail wags the rational dog." (Jonathan Haidt 2001).

1.3 Neurobusiness

As we have just noted, there has been a recent dramatic expansion of the fields using neuroscientific research and we would therefore like to create some clarity around the labelling. Indeed we will need to "create" a new term to do real justice to the variety of related disciplines that have sprung up in recent years.

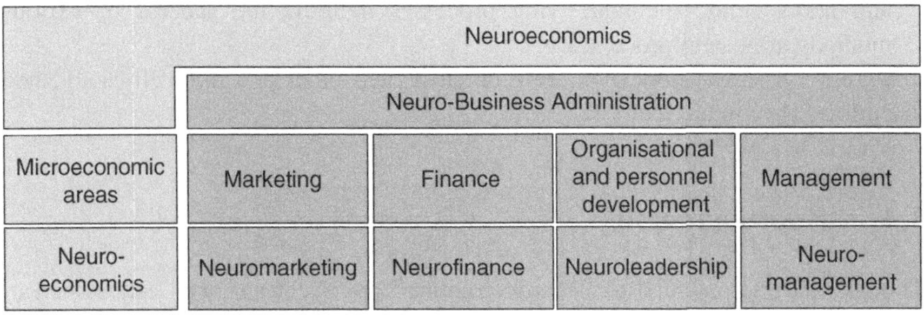

Neuroeconomics				
	Neuro-Business Administration			
Microeconomic areas	Marketing	Finance	Organisational and personnel development	Management
Neuro-economics	Neuromarketing	Neurofinance	Neuroleadership	Neuro-management

Fig. 1.2 Neuroeconomics

Looking into the disciplines that have developed in recent years, we have neuromarketing, neurofinance, neuroleadership and neuromanagement but in addition more and more terms are popping up in various locations and through various sources such as: neurocoaching, neurocommunication and neurostrategy. The standard form of taking a term such as "strategy" and adding "neuro" to it shows that the discipline itself is strongly grounded in the "old" discipline and that the discipline itself is not totally new. This means, therefore, that the discipline of marketing is not changing, but rather the way we are going about it and the tools that we use are changing with the access to the science of the brain.

This, we feel, means that we need to propose the new overriding term of "*Neuro-Business Administration*" to define the fields which all fall under the standard field of business administration. This will all fall under the umbrella of economics (microeconomics). The current disciplines which have a sustainable body of research and practitioners to warrant them being labelled separately and being defined as a separate field are:

- **Neuromarketing** looks into the brain to understand the influences of marketing and how these can be better directed. This by nature looks into the processes and decision making constructs in the brains of the consumer faced with decisions to buy or not and also in contexts of brand building.
- **Neurofinance** researches the neuronal processes of fictive financial transactions. The goal here is to find the driving motives and processes involved in financial decision making involving risk and looking into the neuronal correlates of transactional success or failure.
- **Neuroleadership** is focussed on organisational and personnel related topics. Specifically how the brain, the underlying neuronal processes are involved in and with the interactions of employees and their leaders.
- **Neuromanagement** looks into the brain processes that are driving the management processes in a company. This moves from a personal to a personnel level

and helps define the underlying processes defining the success of various methods, tools and processes.[1]

Figure 1.2 shows how each are related to each other and the well-established disciplines they relate to.

1.4   Neuroleadership

Though some terms such as "neuromarketing" are becoming well established in marketing circles the term "neuroleadership", in contrast, has yet to break fully into management and leadership terminology and practices. This, we believe, is mostly due to the lack of concrete actions and broader specific applications in daily business life. Neuromarketing in comparison has direct applications in changing how a corporation markets, places or sells a product. Marketing professionals have also immediately seen the relevance of looking into the brain as a source for information on how to best tap into the needs and desires of consumers. Neuromarketing is directly linked to the brain of consumers and hence their motives for buying. Marketers indeed have for years been interested in finding out more about human behaviour and how to influence this in contexts of buying and branding. Leadership is, however, a much broader field and even organisational psychology has always taken a back seat to organisational structure, processes and strategy. The goals of business are directed towards producing a product or service and though leadership training is given a portion of focus it is only a portion.

As we write this neuroscientific research is producing a wealth of knowledge around the brain combined with motives of human beings in many contexts—many of these contexts are directly applicable to businesses. Yet the many facets of leadership and the plethora of skills and competencies implicated in successful leadership make it a complex area to apply the learning and knowledge from neuroscience that is being harvested day by day. We feel it is but a question of time before this will be taken up by business after business in all areas of operation. If business focuses on human interactions, then knowledge of the brain can impact this and help to define the solutions to the many problems that businesses are continually faced with. First however, we need to understand what exactly neuroleadership does—what it is.

Neuroleadership in its simplest form is the application of methods and knowledge from neuroscience and how we understand the human brain works in given business contexts. Concretely we can now look into the brain and understand how human beings are acting, reacting and interacting in business contexts. This knowledge can give us clear insights and tools to make people processes and the work environment more brain friendly. Our research and analysis of the current state of knowledge lead us to highlight the following points:

---

[1] Robert Branche reports in his book in French "Neuromanagement" on his experiences and research on the topic of neuromanagement during his work.

- Neuroscience can point to underlying neurological processes of human behaviour and hence we can understand what is influencing and also how to influence this behaviour.
- Research in neuroscience and neuropsychotherapy highlights four basic human needs. These four basic needs, we believe, are the key pillars of neuroleadership in a broader context because only by fulfilling and keeping the basic needs in harmony can a person's brain operate effectively, efficiently and use its full potential (see Chap. 4).
- To achieve harmony between the basic needs we can effectively use instruments and tools from organisational development, personnel development and leadership practices to design a brain friendly and individualistic environment for employees. This will put employees' brains in an optimal state for optimal performance.

In the following chapters we will look, in more detail, into what neuroscience tells us about human behaviour and how we can take this and apply it in the business environment. Neuroleadership can be defined as leading one's own and other people's brains. However in a broad organisational context and the focus of this book we will define neuroleadership as:

Creating a working environment that stimulates and harmonises employees' four basic needs of the brain.

1.5 Defining the Nature of Human Nature: Historical Concepts of Man

The findings that have come from neuroscientific research have also shaken up the concept of man; our view of human beings, and man's respective motives and drives. Neuroscience has furthermore also questioned the concept of consciousness, morality, choice and even free will—we are now able to look much deeper at what these are and the results are sometimes surprising and counter intuitive and hard for many to come to terms with. We after all do not like to think of ourselves without a free will (or with extremely limited free will).

The historical concept of man and his motives is therefore being reshaped by science. This is important because business and organisational psychology takes into account the type of person we are dealing with whether that be the consumer or the employee. Business concepts are defined around this concept, around the person interacting in the field of business whether we are trying to lead them or sell to them. This concept of man and his motives is also what has driven economic theory in many forms. Historically we can see four clear and distinct stages of perception of man and we are now entering the fifth phase—that of "brain-directed man". However, many theories still at large rely on some of the older models—homo economicus specifically which seems to have been forged deeply into perceptions and it is a stubborn concept which is hard to wipe out of our consciousness.

1.5.1 Homo Economicus: Economic Man

Our view of man has always been food for philosophers particularly in the days before we had dreamt of the word economics. Plautus the Roman playwright gave Latin the proverb of "Homo homini lupus est"—"man is a wolf to man". This was drawn on again by the British philosopher Thomas Hobbes who also declared that man was a power hungry egoistic being. The utility power seeking man we can see at the start of the 16th Century with Machiavelli's "The Prince" bringing the term Machiavellian into our language for this type of behaviour. With the advent of Adam Smith we have developed this theory into a more positive economic being (that ultimately benefits society). Smith notes in his magnum opus "The Wealth of Nations": "It is not from the benevolence of the butcher, the brewer, or the baker, that we expect our dinner, but from their regard to their own interest" (Smith 1904). From this developed the modern figure of homo economicus, economic man. This, in more recent times, is firmly grounded in the work of the Frederick Winslow Taylor (1856–1915), the father of scientific management whose work was greatly influential—it is hard to overestimate its importance.

Taylor aimed, with his studies and application of science, to help corporations achieve higher performance through systemic use of employees using scientifically proven methods and in addition to improving the quality of life of workers through higher pay (because of increased productivity). His, now legendary, paper "The Principles of Scientific Management" (Taylor 1911) was extremely influential and probably helped shape management thinking for almost a century. His theories were based on the viewpoint that man was only interested in economic advantage and could only be motivated through financial means—the classic homo economicus. Furthermore he believed that irrational behaviour of man is in main due to lack of self-discipline and this must be controlled by others (giving birth to excessive management control).

Employee's Initiation in Scientific Management (Taylor 1911)
"Well, if you are a high-priced man, you will do exactly as this man tells you tomorrow, from morning till night. When he tells you to pick up a pig and walk, you pick it up and you walk, and when he tells you to sit down and rest, you sit down. You do that right straight through the day. And what's more, no back talk. Now a high-priced man does just what he's told to do, and no back talk. Do you understand that? When this man tells you to walk, you walk; when he tells you to sit down, you sit down, and you don't talk back at him. Now you come on to work here tomorrow morning and I'll know before night whether you are really a high-priced man or not."

Taylor's goals were indeed honourable—he aimed to increase productivity and to help fight the challenges that industry faced and to do this he believed in a scientific approach. Taylor was the first man in recorded history to consider systematic observation of work processes and from this developed concepts of the division of labour and strict working regimes with clear instructions, processes and intensive control.

Taylor's view was that man is a machine and that this must be controlled and hence he aimed to shift the power from the workers to management and to systems in production. His principles did indeed help to increase productivity, especially in the car industry and it was this that influenced and drove the implementation of the assembly lines (and not just Ford as popularly believed). He also drove strongly the empirical side to management research.

This in turn influenced many subsequent practitioners in the field and also economists and in turn led to the solidification of the utility maximising being that homo economicus represents and is indeed the fundamental of most economic theory. The term itself was, incidentally, first used in the late 19th century by John Stuart Mill in his work on political economy (Persky 1995).

This view was representative of the concept of man, a worldview even, at the time and also of strong social segregation. Taylor noted that a man who chose to work forging pig iron, for example, would be too stupid to be able to understand the scientific foundation of its formation. This attitude prevailed for decades—that workers should not and could not be informed of deeper and larger processes. It arguably is also deeply embedded in the trade union vs. management split and is still present in current worker and management relations in many industries and in national politics. Homo economicus, utility seeking man, was the driving premise of much economic theory from Taylor's time, and through much of the 20th century, Lionel Robbins' Rational Choice Theory (Backhouse and Medema 2009) came to dominate economic theory. This also in turn fed the concept of homo economicus as the man who acted rationally on knowledge to increase his own utility—to increase his own personal wealth in short. This belief has indeed become deeply embedded in much economic theory despite many revisions to the concept of man.

Ironically, as a side note, some of Taylor's statements are, maybe, prescient to the larger future of management: he argued that the focus must be on training rather than finding the right man and that the first goal of good systems should be in developing first-class men. Something that can be found, for example, deeply embedded in the much-admired General Electric focus on training, people and leadership development.

1.5.2 Homo Sociologicus—Social Man

The human relations movement (Bruce 2006) which developed out of George Elton Mayo's Hawthorne studies in the early 1930s are considered by many to be the counterpoint to Taylorism and scientific management. The human relations movement brought the worker to the forefront and the worker was acknowledged as a social being and it was understood that interpersonal relationships were important for the workplace. There sprung forth a belief that productivity was not a machine-like mechanism but came also from an internal drive and deeper need of employee satisfaction which in turn led to increased motivation and productivity. It fundamentally saw human beings as just this and not as machines.

The starting point of this was the now fabled Hawthorne studies (Mayo 1949) in the 1930s. The Hawthorne studies were carried out at the Western Electric Company in Hawthorne, Chicago between 1924 and 1930. These studies were commissioned to research the effects of various environmental factors in increasing motivation and worker satisfaction. The surprising take away of these studies was not that the various factors such as increased lighting and cleaner workplaces increased productivity but rather the fact that the workers were being studied seemed to be the cause of the increase in productivity: productivity increased during the study but dropped after the study and this increase in productivity was also observed in the control group. This is the Hawthorne Effect which states that study subjects change their behaviour because they are being researched. The Hawthorne Effect is still taken into consideration in modern day science and the studies themselves are to this day quoted in management literature.

The deeper understanding is that the interest in the workers also drove productivity and in short that employees believing that management cared improved their motivation and productivity. Furthermore the studies also highlighted how workers cooperate with each other (sometimes against management)—in the famous Bank Wiring Room experiments specifically. Here increased incentives actually lowered productivity due to scepticism of the corporate motives. It highlighted that workers had formal and non-formal cliques and these would strongly influence each other's behaviours and level of conforming to management policy. This highlighted that a work environment was not a mechanical environment where people went about their work like machines but rather that various social forms, interactions and influences were an influential part of the workplace.

Indeed much criticism has followed with various interpretations of the results of the Hawthorne studies. Yet though there may be many interpretations of the results, they were instrumental in showing that there ware various driving forces affecting motivation, job satisfaction, workplace performance, productivity and even predictability of workers' suitability for a job. This is why they are so important. Man had become a social being that responds to social stimuli. The worker was now a social machine.

1.5.3 Self-Actualising Man

The self-actualising man is that being that follows its own self-development and looks to fulfil higher needs and develop into a better being. To become something bigger and better and ultimately to reach a level of actualisation dealing with bigger and more abstract concepts in life including spirituality and morality.

This was driven strongly by Abraham Maslow's work after the Second World War. Much of his work paved the way for a different form of psychology that was not necessarily focused on the sick and deficient. Indeed much of positive psychology has its roots in Maslow's work. Maslow's pyramid is the schematic representation of his work (Maslow 1943). The four lower levels of the pyramid represent the deficit needs. The needs are meant to be fulfilled in this order:

- Physiological needs such as food, drink, shelter, sex
- Safety needs such as law and order, security of job and resources
- Love and belonging needs within family and friends
- Esteem needs such as self esteem, achievement and respect by others

If these needs have been fulfilled then come the developmental needs at the next highest level: the self-actualisation needs. These are the higher sphere of needs and represent areas such as morality, creativity, problem solving, and lack of prejudice. Maslow's pyramid has become a classic in itself and is quoted in management literature and self-development books the world over even though this is based on his own personal experience and has not been scientifically validated. The theory is compelling and seems to have an inherent logic that many feel to be correct and this is why it is so popular to this day.

1.5.4 Complex Man

These views of man, however, have all been limited and one-dimensional with single, or limited, motivational drivers: man driven by money, man driven by social needs, man driven by a series of specific needs. This is obviously an over simplification and gives corporations only limited dimensions to work with in the working place.

Complex man can be ascribed to the work of Edgar H. Schein, one of the fathers of modern organisational development, the term *corporate culture* is also attributed to him. Schein looked long and hard at the views we have of man: "the nature of human nature" as he called it (Schein 1980). The view of the complex man aims to take into account this complexity and do some sort of justice to human beings. These are the assumptions that underlie the complex man:

- Complex man has different motives which can change depending on the situation. These are influenced by the current personal situation and stage of development. This will be different from person to person.
- On the basis of organisational experience each employee is capable of learning and applying this to new situations.
- Employees will react differently to management strategies and motives. This means that there is no one management strategy that can lead to satisfaction and happiness for all people all the time.

Complex man is therefore an ever-changing creature that can and will learn and change behaviour depending on the current situation and environment. This will change over time and different parts of the population. This reflects the nature of human nature. Seymour Lieberman noted in 1956 (Lieberman 1956) that we can change our motivations in the short term according to external circumstances and that they are not driven by one single overriding motive. Daniel Kahnemen's Nobel Prize winning work also breaks the model of the homo economicus and takes a more irrational and flexible model of human nature—Kahneman indeed is a psychologist who through his application of this to economics was awarded the Nobel Prize for Economics for his work (specifically Prospect Theory (Kahneman and Tversky 1979)) in a field he was not trained in.

This has in parallel been supported by a multitude of various psychological models and personality types that have been used in psychometric testing. These have shown a variety of models for personality and are unified in their ability to define humans along various characteristics away from a simple two-step model of human behaviour. The best known of these is the Meyers-Briggs Typology Indicator which defines 16 types of personality (Myers 1962). Though this was not directly applied to the corporate environment further models such as Belbin's Team Roles have also identified eight different team types (Belbin 1981). The list of models and testing tools is currently almost endless it seems. Robert Spillane noted online that the psychometric business is reportedly valued at $500 million with up to 92% of organisations using psychometric testing in recruiting (Spillane 2012). This burst in psychometric and personality testing, though not giving full justice to complex man, shows a fundamental shift in mental paradigms. The corporate world is realising that there are a variety of personality types and not one or two. These will have different skills but also different drives and motivations and different reactions to given situations. But these types of tests still all too often box people into a specific type. The complex man theory is more than a variety of types. It is the whole spectrum of types across a multitude of motives, motivations and drives which are ever changing. Complex man theory does not define human beings into limited types it is the full spectrum of human beings and their behaviours.

For corporations this means moving away from the boxing in of people in rigid personality types or single types. This will also mean creating more flexible working environments. This also raises the stakes for management as their role in managing and developing this complex mass of humanity and forming these into more productive and better human beings may pose many challenges. It means reacting to different people in different ways and brings more complexity to management than ever before.

1.5.5 Brain-Directed Man

Whereby the complex man is, as the name implies, complex this gives rise to many challenges in organisational development and in management as mentioned. Dealing with complexity is after all one of the main challenges of corporations, who by nature will try to create simplified processes and structures to decrease complexity, to find solutions to problems, increase productivity and lower costs. Indeed the concept of the complex man directly influenced and helped form Peter Senge's "The Fifth Discipline, the art and practice of the learning organisation" (Senge 2004). Senge saw many problems in corporations: the lack of systems thinking, inability to learn and ascribing problems to the wrong causes. Yet though considered a seminal work[2] John Van Maurik observed "...it is a matter of great regret" "that more organizations have not taken his advice and have remained geared to the quick fix".

---

[2] It did sell millions of copies in book form and was rated by the Harvard Business Review in 1997 as one of the seminal managment books of the previous 75 years.

(Van Maurik 2001). Somehow the idea of a learning organisation is too soft and ever changing for organisations to be able to get to grips with.

This leads us on to where brain science fits in nicely in this equation. With the latest research in neuroscience and all its related fields such as cognitive neuroscience and many more (see Chap. 2) we have never before had so much understanding of human behaviour at such a concrete level. The insights into brain science are showing clearly and powerfully how human beings are operating and how their brain functions can be applied to behaviours and motivations. We can now look into the brain and see what parts of the brain are lighting up and draw powerful conclusions to human behaviour. The research into the brain is enormous, driven along many axis: medical research into ailments such as Alzheimer's, evolutionary, biological sciences, behavioural sciences, artificial intelligence and so on and so forth. The brain is being researched day by day in a variety of contexts. This means the research is rich and broad. More than that some of the insights are giving us more concrete understandings of these behaviours and this clarity is appealing to corporations and managers because it takes the softness out of the soft sciences and indeed takes this into the hard science of biology. It is not soft and elusive but hard biological fact, we can see the pictures and read the research and make extensive theories of human behaviour.

- Human behaviour stems from the brain. We can identify various brain regions that influence certain types of behaviour. Behaviour is not based on rationality but rather on various motives that stem from interaction of various brain regions which have significance for the human being. Furthermore various underlying patterns and triggers are deeply programmed which have been layered on through the various experiences starting from birth on. This gives rise to an individual and complex structure of motives and motivations which we can however gain some clear insight into (see Sects. 2.7 and 4.1).
- Emotions are affective drivers for behaviour and these emotions lie over most cognitive processes to a greater or lesser extent. The rational processes can influence an emotional feeling but tend to have a secondary impact (see Sect. 2.7).
- The fulfilment of the neuroscientific basic needs is essential for employee satisfaction. Various factors will affect the relevance and importance of these needs at any given time (see Sect. 4.1).

The research is now showing a confirmation of the view of man that we have developed over time—complex man is the reality and rationality actually takes a secondary role in human motives and behaviours. We can also see that organisational and personnel management have direct impacts on the way the human being operates and reacts to the environment:

- Behaviours create and solidify brain circuits—the environment forms the brain. In change processes we need to understand the neural processes, as we will be fighting against neuronally wired pathways.
- Human basic needs lie at the heart of the personal interaction with the environment and personal behaviours. Environments that are not in harmony with human basic needs of the individual will cause deficient behaviour.

Concept of Man	Economic man	Social man	Self-actualising man	Complex man	Brain-directed man
Year	1900	1930	1950	1960	2000
Type of being	Machine-like being	Social being	Being with need for development	Facet-rich being	Brain-focused being
Behavioural and decision making processes	Controlled and cognitive processes form behaviours and decision-making processes.				Emotions lie over cognitive processes
Source of motivation	Financial stimuli	Social stimuli	Unfulfilled needs on the hierarchical levels of needs	Variety of sources depending on person and situation	Complex structure based on the underlying neural substrates
Consequences for working processes	Optimising working processes	Improve social environment	Increase autonomy and free room	Complex motivational structure	Satisfaction of neuroscientific basic needs; activation of personal reward systems

Fig. 1.3 Overview of concepts of man

- Base human motivational drives will be driven by the manifestation of the desire to fulfil or protect human basic needs. Therefore to tap into potential, motivation at a deeper intrinsic level we need to understand the basic needs and how they are represented and fulfilled by each individual (Fig. 1.3).

1.6 Summary

- The current understanding of neuroeconomics can be defined in a specific and a broader concept:
  - Neuroeconomics in a specific sense is focused on the classic microeconomic questions.
  - Neuroeconomics in a broader context included all scientific research into the neuronal bases of our interactions in the economy as whole.
- We propose the term "**neuro business administration**" which, in parallel to business administration, focuses on all issues around administrating businesses but through using research into the brain to support the theories, concepts and paradigms that are produced.
- Neuroleadership:
  - Leading one's own and other's brains
  - Satisfying the four neuroscientific *basic needs*
  - The goal of management and administration is to strive for *harmony* with basic needs, the brain and the working environment.
- The research into the brain has created the new (and final?) model of the *brain-directed man*:
  - Experience drives current behaviour and these patterns form a complex structure of motives and motivations.
  - Is always capable of change and learning

Neuroscience for Business

2

The brain and the neurosciences may be an unexplored field for many readers and so we aim in this chapter to jump into some of the specifics of the brain: to understand how it develops, how it functions and what this means for us. We will start with a very brief history of neuroscience before moving into the brain and its formation and functioning. We will then throw a spotlight on the technology that is driving the research before moving in to some specifics of brain functions that have a key impact on business and how we operate.

Objectives

- Understand the different fields in neuroscience
- Provide an overview of the technologies behind the research
- Understand the brain's structure
- Introduction to key biological substrates of the brain
- A basic functional understanding of the brain and impact on business contexts

2.1   Introduction

The neurosciences are far-reaching and interdisciplinary in their nature. Indeed, they need to be if they want to look into the functioning of the nervous system as a whole. This includes the biology but also the psychology and not forgetting the body itself. Neuroscientists need to be thinking at a molecular level but also at a human behavioural level. There have been massive steps in the neurosciences in recent years and our knowledge of the brain has made huge leaps forward and this has also opened the doors for wider applications in and out of the laboratory meaning that many disciplines now come under the umbrella of the neurosciences. This chapter serves to give an overview and introduction to the neurosciences and the brain.

A. Ghadiri et al., *Neuroleadership*, Management for Professionals,
DOI 10.1007/978-3-642-30165-0_2, © Springer-Verlag Berlin Heidelberg 2012

2.2   Neuroscience: its Development and its Disciplines

2.2.1   A Very Brief History of Neuroscience

The history of neuroscience in many ways is linked tightly to the history of medicine but also to perceptions of man: the idea that our consciousness could sit in an organ was anathema to many religions.

Trepanation, the act of boring or scraping a hole in the skull to relieve pressure due to damage, has been found in many Neolithic cultures (Heidecker 2006) and is still practised in some remote tribes in Africa. Some knowledge of brain damage has been recorded by Egyptians dating back to 1700 BC (Kandel et al. 2000). However, the predominant view in the ancient world was that the heart was the source of consciousness though Hippocrates challenged this noting the proximity to the sensory organs. Aristotle was unconvinced and still espoused the heart as the seat of consciousness and the brain as simply a cooling mechanism for blood. It was only Galen a Roman physician who noted the effects of a damaged brain on gladiators. Galen himself was a skilled surgeon—many of his techniques would not be used until centuries later and some are precursors to today's operations (for example his cataract operations). His "squealing pig operation" was likely the first experimental evidence that the brain is connected to action (Gross 1998).

Further advances were made in the Middle Ages with ever increasing skills of surgeons and the continual study of dissections. Some names in the brain, the hippocampus, for example, date back to this era (Gurunluoglu et al. 2011).

The well-known case of Phineas Gage in 1848, though it is in actuality poorly documented, showed that there were potentially regional functions in the brain linked to personality disorders (Bigelow and Barnard 2002). This had been proposed by Gall in the eighteenth century (but discredited by many including the Roman Catholic Church who thought that God creating a physical seat of the mind, which was God-given, as being an anathema) (Gall and Spurzheim 1810). Phineas Gage was a foreman working on railroad construction and in a bizarre accident a metal rod was blasted through his head—under his cheek bone, taking out his right eye and up through the front part of the skull. He survived, miraculously, and recovered, but apparently suffered severe personality disruptions. Around this period there was more research from physicians such as Broca and Wernicke whose study of patients with tumours led them to identify two different areas involved in language production and language comprehension respectively.

Neuroscience, however, took a large step forward with the development of the microscope and at the turn of the twentieth century Cajal's study of neurons using Golgi's method of staining tissue using silver nitrate—this is still the base of various tissue staining techniques used to this day—led to the first pictorial representations of neurons (Jones 2007). Cajal detailed diagrams of neurons led to the development of the theory of the neuron—the neuron as the base for interactions in the brain (Tixier-Vidal 2010).

At the same time it was also proposed that neurons were electrically excitable. The localization theory was further supported by the work of John Hughlings

Jackson whose work into epilepsy patients led him to correctly infer the organisation of the motor cortex. Brodmann published his map of the brain in 1909 (Brodmann 1909; Loukas et al. 2011) labelling different areas. His numbered areas are still used today e.g. Brodmann area 4 is the primary motor cortex.

In 1952 Andrew Huxley first proposed a mathematical model for the electrical currents, action potentials, in neurons (Hodgkin and Huxley 1952) and in 1962 the transmission across synapses—between neurons—was first modelled by Bernhard Katz (Cowen & Kandel 2001). Eric Kandel's famous work into memory started in 1966 and from this time we saw neuroscience as an ever-expanding field.

The 1980s saw more popular books such as Oliver Sacks' "The Man who Mistook is Wife for a Hat" (Sacks 1985) bringing brain disorders into the public spotlight. With the advent of imaging technologies in the 1980s and 1990s (the 1990s were also declared the decade of the brain which stimulated substantial government funding, particularly in the USA) the research has mushroomed with ever increasing fields also looking into the brain. This is not least also driven by major pharmaceutical companies taking a great interest with the rise of disorders such as Alzheimer's, Parkinson's and dementia. We now have a mass of information and thousands of institutions with the latest technology looking into the brain at different levels and as this increases so does the funding and the technology. Though we have gained deep insights and made large steps in understanding, the brain's sheer complexity makes many processes still very elusive. Some claim we know enough to, for example, build a model of a brain in a computer (Blue Brain Project at EPFL in Lausanne (Blue Brain Project)[1], Switzerland) to simulate sicknesses and disorders and simulate the functions of drugs in the brain, others claim we have but scratched the surface.

But first let us look into what the neurosciences actually consist of, what the disciplines are.

2.2.2 Neuroscientific Disciplines

As we mentioned previously the neurosciences cover a large area and to the laymen these may sound similar and yet the differences for us are important. We will therefore now outline the terminology and formal disciplines in the neurosciences. Figure 2.1 represents an overview of these disciplines.

1. **Neurology**
   Neurology is the discipline of dealing with disorders of the nervous system and is a part of human medicine. This means specifically dealing with the diagnosis, therapy and prevention of sickness in the nervous system. This includes disorders in the central, peripheral and vegetative nervous system.

2. **Neurobiology**
   Neurobiology is the study of the structure, function and development of nerve cells and the nervous system. The term neurobiology is sometimes, however,

---

[1] http://bluebrain.epfl.ch/ Accessed 1 Nov 2012]

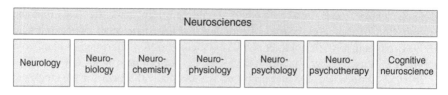

Fig. 2.1 Disciplines of neuroscience

used interchangeably with neuroscience whereby neurobiology is the specific study of the brain and its biological functions. Neuroscience is the broader science of the whole nervous system.

3. **Neurochemistry**

   Neurochemistry is the study of the chemical processes at a cellular level in the nervous system. The main focus is on the chemical transmitters in the synapses and the function of the receptors. The function of the neuroendocrine (hormone) system is also a key focus of neurochemistry.

4. **Neurophysiology**

   Neurophysiology is a sub-discipline of physiology and is the study of the performance and reaction of our nervous system to external stimuli. The focus is on the dynamic processes between nerve cells and how these process information.

5. **Neuropsychology**

   Neuropsychology is the study at the interface of psychology and the neurosciences. Here neuropsychologists will study behaviour in combination with neuroscientific technologies. For example, a decision-making task will also be analysed using brain scanning to identify which areas are activated in making specific choices. The goal is to connect behaviour to various brain regions and their specific processing and functions.

6. **Neuropsychotherapy**

   Neuropsychotherapy uses neuroscientific insights to treat psychological disorders. This is driven by the understanding that brain forms its view of the world through structural communication in the brain and that dysfunction in personality can also be represented by dysfunctions in the biology of the brain. The biology of the brain also shows that the brain is plastic and so new pathways and ways of behaving can be formed and reformed. In addition neuropsychotherapy aims to understand the chemical processes in the brain and how these manifest in different cognitive processes and are also biologically linked through the brain's ability to build respective receptors to these chemicals (see Sect. 2.9.1).

7. **Cognitive Neuroscience**

   Cognitive neuroscience deals with the neural substrates of cognition, of mental processes. They may include studying the neural mechanisms involved in attention, reward, memory and fear. Cognitive neuroscientists are instrumental in mapping the brain and its regions based on its cognitive functions.

   This overview shows how many fields are included in the broad context of neuroscience and many of these overlap and indeed many research teams may have different specialists on the team. This is necessary as the brain is incredibly complex with a host of biological, chemical and cognitive processes all functioning in parallel to give rise to various psychiatric or nervous system disorders.

2.3   The Brain

The brain, it may seem obvious, plays a central role in the neurosciences. It is we note not the only focus as the central nervous system also includes all nerves in the body and there is also a growing body of research into embodied cognition: how thought can be grounded in the body and how the body can influence cognition— but for the purposes of this book we will not enter into this fascinating area. The brain we can see as the central processing unit of human beings. It is the seat of consciousness, of memory and hence also our feeling of "self" on top of our sensory and cognitive interaction with the world. The brain is therefore, in no short part, what we are. Its importance in the organism itself can also be seen by the amount of power and energy it uses:

Some facts and figures about the brain
- *The average human brain weighs 1.3 Kg and is 80 % water.*
- *The brain is only 2 % of body weight but uses up to 25 % of the body's energy resources (water, oxygen and glucose).*
- *The brain consists of around 100 billion neurons with 100 trillion connections between each other.*
- *Up to 1,200 litres of blood flow through the brain each day delivering up to 70 litres of oxygen.*
- *The left hemisphere deals with facts and details. The specifics of language, vocabulary and grammar also sit here.*
- *The right hemisphere has broader connections to emotions, empathy but importantly to the holistic and big picture view of the world.*

Some myths about the brain
The brain is fixed in size and does not change over life—many changes happen and due to neuroplasticity the brain is ever changing.

Alcohol kills brain cells—alcohol disrupts the firing patterns of the brain's neurons but does not kill brain cells (only in extreme over-indulgence).

Intelligence is genetic—intelligence is partly genetic but is more linked to ability to connect and draw on various resources in the brain.

Reason and rationality are separate to emotionality—the emotional centres of the brain operate together with emotionality taking a driving seat.

Behaviours are hard-wired—we have many instinctive reactions that are hard-wired but many behaviours are linked to our interaction with the environment.

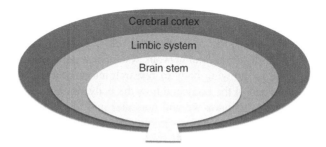

Fig. 2.2 Three-layer model of the brain

The brain is a complex organ with 100 billion neurons, brain cells that is, connected together in different formations and regions. In fact this seems so complex that it seems an illusion to believe we can understand the details and their subsequent influences on the rest of the brain and organism as a whole. Indeed it has been calculated that the number of possible connections in the brain is greater than the number of atoms in the universe. This may indeed be just popular science but it demonstrates, more than anything else, the sheer complexity of the brain. Yet when we look at the brain we can clearly see different structures and forms and we start to see that there is structure in the complexity. Like a country with millions of people who live in different households and in different villages and towns which are connected in different ways with paths, roads and highways. So it is with our brain. We can also see a general grouping of structures that simplifies the view of the brain even further. Though technically speaking neurobiologists speak of five regions, the three-layer model from the American brain researcher MacLean (see Fig. 2.2) is one that is simple and is generally speaking closely linked to reality (MacLean 1990). Though, we note, in the literature there is some discrepancy as to what structures actually belong to each, we can think of the brain in terms of

- The brain stem
- The limbic system
- The cerebral cortex

We will briefly look at these three areas and we will then draw attention to a number of structures that are particularly relevant to us in the context of neuroleadership.

2.3.1 Brain Stem

The brain stem is at the top of the spinal cord (including the upper part of the spinal cord) and the so-called small brain and back brain (cerebellum). This is the oldest part of the brain in an evolutionary sense. It is sometimes called the reptilian brain or the old brain. This part of the brain controls the incoming signals from the spine as well as basic reflexes and homeostasis—living that is: heartbeat, breathing, etc.

An important part of the brain stem is the thalamus (this is sometimes categorised in the limbic system). This is like a relay station for the sensory inputs.

All sensory inputs will pass though the thalamus and the thalamus does the first basic sorting and sending of signals to other parts of the brain. The thalamus is connected directly to the outer cortex, to the amygdale (emotional processing units) and to the hippocampus (for memory consolidation). In short the thalamus decides what information needs to be processed and at what level: unconscious or conscious. In some sense then the thalamus is a key centre for your consciousness, or at least awareness of the environment around us (the subject of consciousness is much debated by neuroscientists and philosophers alike).

2.3.2   The Limbic System

The limbic system is the next layer of the onion so to speak. It lies directly over the brain stem, deep inside the brain. It is, from an evolutionary perspective, the next oldest part of the brain and is sometimes called the inner cortex, the old mammalian brain or the middle brain. The limbic system has to some extent been popularised by much recent publicity in many popular books on person, and personality. Indeed it is of central importance because the limbic system is the emotional centre in our brain and processes a wide range of emotions (Bruce & Braford 2009; Ploog 1980; LeDoux 1991; Isaacson et al. 2001).

The limbic system is also tightly connected to the brain stem and particularly to the **hypothalamus** which plays a key role in linking the nervous system to the endocrine system—the hormonal system—via the pituitary gland. The hypothalamus controls various primitive impulses such as hunger and thirst but also body temperature, fatigue and sleep. It therefore has a role of putting our emotions into feelings (Brooks 1988).

The important structures in the limbic system are:

The **amygdala** (plural is amygdalae but it is in general used in the singular) are two small almond-shaped structures sitting deep in the brain and are considered our emotional processing units (the name stems from the Greek word for almond). Though they can be separated into different areas responsible for different functions their relevance to fear processing has been particularly intensively researched. The amygdalae are widely connected to other brain regions hence the importance of their functioning on the brain. They are considered key units for consolidating body memory because of their importance in processing pain and physical reactions to certain stimuli. This also makes them powerful in the retrieval and formation of somatic markers, emotional triggers that immediately stimulate a series of reactions (Bechara et al. 2003). This also makes them powerful triggers for learning processes (Kilcross 2000). They are however best known for their role in fear processing and their subsequent impact on the brain and body (see Sect. 2.7.2.1) (Davis 1997).

The **hippocampus** is considered the memory centre of the brain. This pair of "seahorse-shaped" (named after the Latin for seahorse) structures sit close to the amygdala. Research into London taxi drivers, for example, who are famed for their extensive and comprehensive memory of street names and the notoriously difficult test to become a Black Cab driver, has shown an increase in the size of the hippocampus (Maguire et al. 2000, Maguire et al. 2006). Some areas of memory such as spatial memory sit in the hippocampus itself. In other contexts the hippocampus seems to have a powerful memory consolidation function (Hynie and Klenerová 1991). Many memories exist as broad networks in the brain (engrams) consolidating, for example, auditory and sensory information also (Schacter 1996). However in absence of the hippocampus we cannot form new memories.

The famous case, in neuroscience circles, is that of HM who in 1959 due to uncontrollable epileptic seizures had parts of his brain removed including the majority of his hippocampus (Squire 2009). He subsequently awoke each day as if yesterday had never happened (the Hollywood film Memento, 2001, portrays a similar case). HM had lost the ability to form new memories and only had memories up to his operation. Since then each day was like the day after his operation. If he met you today and met you again tomorrow, it would be like meeting you again for the first time. (Oliver Sacks in "The Man who Mistook his Wife for a Hat" describes some similar cases but slightly different in nature and in region of the brain damaged (Sacks 1985)).

The **cingulate cortex** lies over the top of the limbic system like an arch and is actually part of the cerebrum, the innermost fold sitting directly on top of the limbic system. It is however considered a part of the limbic system as it closely matches and balances the information in the limbic system. Its functions are closely linked to attention, error detection and monitoring of the environment linking in closely with inputs from the hippocampus and long-term memory. Indeed some enthusiastic researchers claimed in 2008 (ironically meant) that "The cingulate cortex does everything" (Gage et al. 2008).

The **nucleus accumbens** we can consider the brain's reward centre (Wise 2002). Though it is now considered a collection of structures with slightly different functions it broadly processes most forms of reward and is responsible for production of dopamine (from the ventral tegmental area (Saunders and Richard 2011)), our reward hormone in the brain. It will also drive the excretion of oxytocin which is important for trust building and bonding (Liu 2003; Baumgartner et al. 2008). Habit learning patterns and procedural learning patterns are also consolidated here (Setlow 1997). This thus shows the importance of reward in consolidating new habits (see Sect. 2.5.2).

2.3.3 Cerebral Cortex

The cerebral cortex is, from an evolutionary sense, the youngest part of the brain and what is also considered its crowning glory. It is this first and foremost that differentiates us most from other animals and other advanced life forms. We humans have a huge cerebral cortex unmatched in its size and complexity. This is the outermost layer of the brain with deep folds and valleys. It is only a few millimetres thick and in preserved dissected brains is grey in colour, hence the term grey matter. This is also clearly visibly against the white matter, the thick layer that lies beneath this. The white matter is the myleniated axons ("insulted" connections between cells) connecting the cerebral cortex to numerous other areas. This layer is separated into four broad regions "cortices". Each of these perform a cluster of processes that are similar:

- **Occipital cortex**: sitting at the back of the brain and here most of our visual processing sits.
- **Temporal lobes**: sitting at the sides of the brain and where we process abstraction, metaphor and language.
- **Parietal cortex**: sitting over the top of the brain and here we process sensory inputs and coordination in space and time.
- The prefrontal lobes or **prefrontal cortex** (PFC) which is considered the seat of higher functions or executive function. This region is a strong focus in neuroleadership as here sit many of the controlled and conscious processes such as emotional regulation.

In addition to these the motor cortex, which sits like a band over the middle of the brain, is often treated separately to the above-mentioned lobes. The term lobe and cortex is often used interchangeably.

In each of these regions there are various sulci and gyri. Folds and ridges, valley and hills if you wish (sulci are the "valleys" and gyri are the "hills"). These have distinct regions that also have distinct functions which are very similar from person to person. These may be, for example, regions that process sound, visual processing of faces is, for example, closely correlated to one specific region (fusiform face area—FFA (Ganel et al. 2005)). We have centres for language comprehension, Wernicke's area, and for language production, Broca's area. The list is long and these regions are part of the specific focus of many neuroscientists and particularly in cognitive psychology.

Though it is easy to see the three layers of the brain from brain stem, to limbic system to the cerebral cortex as separate functional areas processing living functions, emotional processing and higher functions, these meta regions are all linked together and process information in parallel and with the help of each other. Survival instincts will influence our emotional processing and this will in turn influence our decision-making ability in the cerebral cortex. Or vice versa visual stimuli will be emotionally processed and then lead to an instinctive survival reaction firing strongly from the brain stem. The brain is a powerful interconnected unit and these systems function together to give rise to the multitude of reactions and processes that are part of human beings and what we are and how we function. Indeed until recently we considered the cerebral cortex to be the most important area of the brain where our rationality sits and where the seat of the higher man also sits. Recent work has shown that we are highly emotional beings and that the lower systems can and do control the direction of our thinking rather than the other way around. We are emotional creatures not rational creatures.[2] The brain's power indeed lies in the power of the connections. If we were to tie back the structure of

---

[2] "Descartes' Error" by Antonio Damasio is the now classic book showing that the rationality of Descartes was flawed and that emotions have much more relevance than we could possibly have assumed.

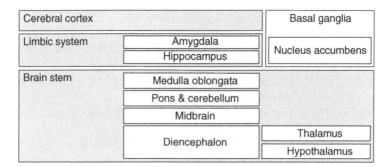

Fig. 2.3 Brain regions

the brain to Camerer's quadrants we would see that only the controlled cognitive processes (I) would be mostly processed in the cerebral cortex (see Fig. 2.1).

Figure 2.3 shows the specific regions in the three-layer model.

2.4   Information Processing in the Brain

The processing scheme of the brain shows how external stimuli are processed and give rise to an action and reaction. The stimuli are first processed in the thalamus and this functions as the first control centre. These signals are then sent further to the amygdala and to specific regions in the cerebral cortex. These stimuli are then balanced and compared to previous experiences and reactions.

These two systems the amygdala (and limbic system) and the cerebral cortex process the information differently and more importantly at different speeds. The amygdala which functions as a central emotional processing unit uses a high-speed reaction circuit which activates immediate emergency reactions. It is the amygdala that stimulates the release of adrenalin after only 12 milliseconds and can therefore immediately increase blood pressure and heart rate and ensure that the reaction ability of the body is intact (McIntyre et al. 2003; Davis and Whalen 2001). The cerebral cortex needs more time to form a reaction (a few hundred milliseconds, if not seconds) but it is also more precise as this will scan memories and stimuli for more precise information and make a more conscious decision based on the information coming in. You can think of it like this: you walk through a forest and see a coiled up shape on the ground. As you mind says "snake" you will likely jump back, your body will be energised and you will be ready to flee: your senses will have immediately focused and you will have heightened attention. This is the quick processing path, the emotional/amygdala path. Yet as you look closer you see that this coil is only a rope someone has left lying there and your more detailed processing sees this and our body will relax as we comprehend that it is only a rope and nothing to be worried about. This is your cerebral cortex focusing on more detail and coming to a more detailed analysis of the situation. You will likely laugh–which is a primal reaction to stress and this in turn will release calming hormones.

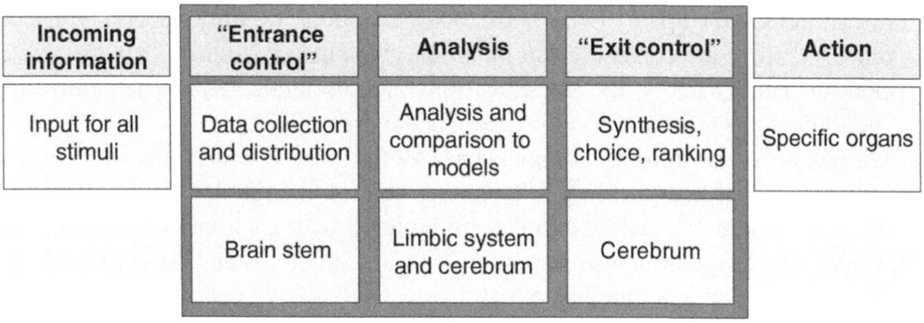

Incoming information	"Entrance control"	Analysis	"Exit control"	Action
Input for all stimuli	Data collection and distribution	Analysis and comparison to models	Synthesis, choice, ranking	Specific organs
	Brain stem	Limbic system and cerebrum	Cerebrum	

Fig. 2.4 Processing scheme in the brain (based on Seidel 2004, p 41)

Both of these centres work together and collaborate to come to better decisions as in the above example of the rope. They compliment each other—the primal amygdala reaction path protecting us and the cerebral cortex contributing to our higher functions and more detailed processing. Ultimately the cerebrum (specifically the preforntal cortex) can act as the director and can exert control over our actions and reactions (see Fig. 2.4) (Miller and Cohen 2001; Banks et al. 2007; Ochsner and Gross 2005).

2.5   Important Insights

In recent years there have been many breakthroughs in neuroscience and the research and number of reports have exploded—this can leave many who take an interest in neuroscience with a feeling of confusion and an inability to know where to start. For leaders and laymen it is even worse. We would therefore like to, from this plethora of information, draw your attention to a few insights that we find particularly important and relevant in the context of neuroleadership.

- The first important realisation is that of the brain's plasticity. This means the ability of the brain to reform itself and rewire itself. The brain is not as previously believed a fixed structure but rather an ever-changing organism. Specifically the connections between the neurons are forever changing—growing and shrinking according to how much we use the pathways. This means that we can "teach an old dog new tricks" that what is in the brain is not permanent and new learning can always take place (Kolb and Whishaw 1998; Shaw and McEachern 2001).
- The second important realisation is that emotions play a crucial role in these change processes (Rolls 2001). By activating the reward centre in the brain we can stimulate various processes that will contribute to enhanced learning, habit formation and positive emotions in the brain (Nakatani et al. 2009).
- Thirdly the discovery at the start of the 1990s of mirror neurons (see Sect. 2.5.3), that network of neurons across our brain mirroring others actions and that show that we are interconnected at a level never before thought feasible and that these mirror neurons are instrumental in many learning process but also in the reading

of emotions and empathy (Rizzolatti 2008). Emotions are truly infectious. These mirror neurons are considered so important by some researchers that they have been named (namely by the illustrious neuroscientist Ramachandran) the "neurons that shaped civilisation" (Ramachandran 2009).

We will now look into the biological basis of the brain to understand some of the underlying process better and see where they therefore tie into leadership contexts. Learning how neurons function and communicate with each can be particularly relevant for understanding how important learning, emotions and positive working environments are in a corporate context.

2.5.1 Plasticity

Plasticity is the ability of the brain to grow, regrow and reform its connections and functions. Plasticity is the heart of learning and of memory and one of the most important aspects of the brain we would like you to take away. The concept of plasticity is what drives the developing brain and all our learning processes.[3]

In looking into plasticity we need to look at the neuron, the brain cell. The brain has (a staggering) 100 billion neurons[4] and these consist of three main elements: dendrites, cell body and axon (see Fig. 2.5). The cell body is the metabolic centre of the cell. It is where the DNA lies and where all necessary substances for the functioning of the cell are produced. The cell has two types of connections that stretch out like arms or branches on a tree, indeed a neuron can look surprisingly like a tree or indeed a plant with its complex system of roots. The dendrites collect information from other cells. Each cell has numerous dendrites (in some cases up to 50,000 but on average somewhere around 1,000). There is then a single axon which connects to other cells, or specifically their dendrites. The connection between these is not a direct connection but a so-called synapse. The synapses are the connection points of cells yet these do not connect directly—there is a gap called the synaptic cleft. Information is transferred between two different cells through the release of so called neurotransmitters. These are chemicals that are released from the end of the axon, stimulated by the electrical current in the cell. These neurotransmitters then jump over the gap to dock into receptor cells that in turn stimulate another chemical process in the dendrite and send an electrical signal further to the cell body and potentially along the axon and so on and so forth (Kandel 2006). Your thoughts are thousands and millions of these minute chemical processes and electrical impulses (action potentials) travelling at speeds of up to 100 metres per second in the brain.

We now know that the connection process of neurons is very plastic and an ongoing process. The development of the brain in the embryo shows the magic of this process. The brain cells are initially produced in their millions and billions along

---

[3] The free publication "Brain Facts" from the Society for Neuroscience is easy to read, understandable and informative giving the basics of the brain, its development and disorders.

[4] Suzana Herculano-Houzel of the University of Rio de Janeira has put the actual figure at, on average, 86 billion neurons for a male brain.

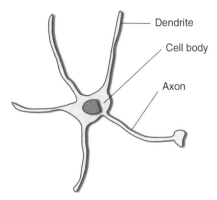

Fig. 2.5 A neuron

the neuronal tube in the primitive brain. These neurons then go through a great migration. They will then "crawl" along glial cells, cells that give structure and provide nutrition and support structures to neurons. The neurons then come to their final locations and once they reach their final location they will try to reach out their arms, dendrites and axons to connect together. We do not know how this neuron migration is coordinated at this time. This is a somewhat magical process whereby millions and billions of neurons migrate to predefined points in the early brain and then start connecting and forming into various regions and structures to give rise to a brain that is surprisingly similar in all humans (indeed in many animals the similarities are astounding) (Carey 2006). Brain cells are programmed to connect to each other. Figure 2.6 illustrates this process.

Another interesting aspect of the neuron formation is that after the cells have found their final place and start communicating to each other there are also various phases of cell death, or cell pruning (the first six months of human life are actually characterised by cell pruning, cell death, and not cell growth as we may falsely have assumed) (Kantor and Kolodkin 2003). Here cells or connections that are not considered important anymore are pared back. This phenomenon has been implicated in our, for example, limited ability in Europe to identify Chinese faces. To us Europeans all Chinese look very similar. And interestingly to Chinese all Europeans look similar. Yet infants have high sensitivity to faces and can identify a much wider variety of differences in similar faces than adults can. Infants of three months are much better at identifying Barbarey Macaques—small monkeys which look extremely similar (their keepers cannot distinguish them). This ability is lost after nine months (Pascalis et al. 2005). The theory is simply that after we find that we do not need our Chinese face neurons these will be culled and we lose the ability to identify Chinese faces and so they all seem similar. The same goes for the Chinese who lose their European face neurons and have trouble identifying European faces even though for Europeans this may seem obscure as we consider ourselves so

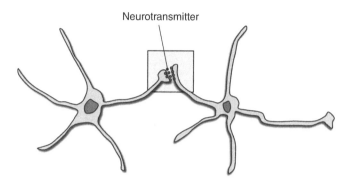

Fig. 2.6 Neurons connecting through a synapse and neurotransmitter

different—but only if we have the neurons that can do this processing. Familiarity over time plays a major role also, obviously, meaning that if we live in China, for example, for a period of time our sensitivity to Chinese faces will increase.

Neuronal learning also highlights this process and in some ways the heart of our learning processing lies at a micro neuronal level. The work of Eric Kandel, Nobel laureate in 2001, showed something powerful.[5] Short-term memory is a chemical process i.e. extended firing of neurons over seconds and minutes that allows us to recall the memory. Long-term memory is a physical process—the stimulation of the brain cells will produce amino acids that will stimulate the growth of new dendrites and will build physical connections—memory is indeed a physical structure. A long-term memory is a physical connection in the brain (Kandel 2006). So any new memory you form means you have changed your brain. This highlights the true power of plasticity for if we are forming new memories, we are rewiring the brain and this above all answers the voices of those sceptics who believe you "cannot teach an old dog new tricks". We can all rewire our brains: any new memory, be it of football match, a new computer programme, a new emotional event, whatever, is a new physical connection in the brain. This is powerful for our purposes in the broader context of neuroleadership.

Another interesting point we need to note when speaking of neuroplasticity is that of neuronal learning. That is, as an organic cell and not a hard electrical circuit, the cell itself learns to distinguish between signals and change it's firing. When a neuron is stimulated with an electrical current there will also be an electrical output. This, however, will not remain stable. If the electrical current is repeated over time repetitively the electrical output will decrease. The cell has learned that this is repetitive and so it creates a *lower* stimulation. This is known as *habituation*. If a few smaller electrical signals are given and then large "shock" signal given, then the following stimuli, the same as the initial small inputs, will give an *increased*

---

[5] Eric Kandel's book "In Search of Memory" is a fascinating read documenting his life and the devleopment of neuroscience and his work after the Second World War.

Fig. 2.7 The three forms
of neuronal learning

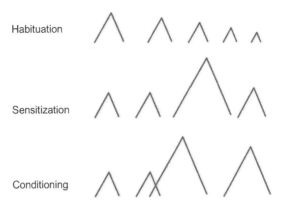

output. This is known as *sensitisation*. Then we come to the classic conditioning
processes whereby a large shock signal is given closely following a small signal.
This small signal will then stimulate a *large* output (Kandel 2006).

This understanding of neuronal learning is important as it shows that our cells
are forever becoming habituated, sensitised and conditioned and that many
concepts that we may class as "psychological" may in fact be grounded in the
biological learning of the cells sitting in our skulls (Kandel and Tauc 1965)
(Fig. 2.7).

The process of developing connections between neurons in the brain can be seen
diagrammatically in Fig. 2.8. The first phase shows how neurons reach out to
connect to each other. The initial connection happens in the second phase and
these cells then start communicating to each other based on the stimuli coming in
leading to stronger pathways in the third phase. If these pathways are continually
used and stimulated this will lead to strong pathways in the fourth phase.

This knowledge of neurons, their connection processes, their learning processes
and the brain's plasticity is extremely important for us. It is extremely important
because this demonstrates that it is our experiences that build our brain. The stimuli
that are coming in and have come into our brains all through our lives have
stimulated various learning and connection processes in the brain and this
influences the way the brain wires together. Our environment and our experiences
do develop our brain (Hüther 2006). It also demonstrates, as we keep mentioning,
that learning something new is always possible. This difficulty lies in the fact that
we may be fighting solid *physical* connections in the brain.

2.5.2   Reward System

The reward system is a complex connection of regions that has now been extensively researched in humans and in animals. The reward system is simply the
system that generates those good feelings. This we now know is generated through
the dopamine system which we can see as the brain's "happy hormone"—it

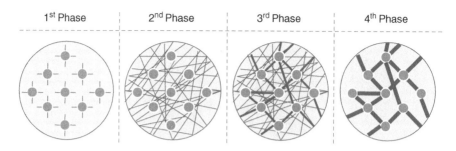

Fig. 2.8 Neuronal connection patterns (Based on Hüther 2006)

stimulates the feeling of happiness and elation (it is, however, we note, involved in many processes) (Arias-Carrión et al. 2010). It is, incidentally, exactly this system that cocaine stimulates.

The earliest research into this system was done on rats (Olds and Milner 1954). Electrodes were implanted in various areas in the brain and the rats could self-stimulate this. It was discovered that in certain areas a feeling of happiness was generated. In some cases this was so intense that these rats would continually keep stimulating the electrodes and neglect to drink or eat.

The dopamine system is now a well-researched system in the brain. Dopamine however is not just reward it has many important functions as a neurotransmitter. It is dopamine that is also essential for attention—our attention system is driven by dopamine but more than that: motivation at a chemical level can be seen as a dopamine process (Nieoullon 2002).

The reward system functions in many ways in humans but researches have split these into two systems of reward: primary and secondary rewards. Primary rewards are those simple survival needs which also generate powerful feelings of reward and happiness and satisfaction. Primary rewards are: food, drink, sex, shelter. This explains our feelings of satisfaction after a good meal and our consistent (and obvious) desire and attention to food and drink. Secondary rewards are rewards that are not directly linked to our primary rewards or only at a secondary level and many arguably help our survival e.g. status shows a primitive level of hierarchy and hence ability to survive and find a suitable mate. Secondary rewards may include:

- Information
- Status
- Acknowledgement
- Gratitude
- Social value
- Altruism
- Trust
- Physical contact

These illustrate more than anything that human beings are driven by many factors and the assumption in many corporations that reward is driven only by money is a fallacy and a dangerous one. Reward and pleasure have a multitude of complex connections and associations (Kringelbach and Berridge 2009). We should note that human beings are intensely social and this is represented also in our reaction to reward, particularly the rewarding experience of social interactions (Adolphs 2003). This may also remind us of the concepts of man we spoke about in the previous chapter—the original homo economicus assuming our only system of reward is financial. The homo sociologicus showed that we were driven by other factors. Indeed this is the strength of the brain-driven model of man because we are now more able than ever to give clearer explanations of the internal motives of man. They are after all represented in the brain. More importantly, reward, attention and motivation are all elements of the dopamine and reward system. Hence many corporations view of motives needs to be reviewed.

The reward system is, however, more than simply reward and motivation, if that is not enough in itself. It is also essential for learning processes particularly habit learning. Positive reinforcement is a key element of learning and this is an element of the reward system. The opposite, fear conditioning, is a form of learning but the impacts are negative and put the body into a state of stress (Nakatani et al. 2009). Tapping into reward is an essential part of this process and one that will drive motivation and collaboration powerfully in any organisation.

Understanding these systems in the brain is important as the neuroleader is a leader that has the ability to understand the brain and understand the deeper drives and therefore is better able to tap into this potential and hence the potential of the workforce and each individual. Understanding individual reward systems will enable the neuroleader to better tap into the powerful drives of motivation and satisfaction of individual employees.

2.5.3   Mirror Neurons

The history of mirror neurons goes back to a neuroscience lab in Parma, Italy of the now illustrious neuroscientist Giacomo Rizzolatti (Rizzolatti 2008). During experiments with monkeys into the function of the motor cortex something unusual happened in a lab situation: a particular monkey had a motor neuron of arm movement wired up to a computer for this particular research. A researcher in the laboratory ate a snack in front of this monkey and as the researcher raised his arm the motor neuron of the monkey activated even though the monkey's arm had not moved. This should not have happened. This, the researcher at first thought, was a faulty reading or that the technical equipment was malfunctioning. It was not. Repeating this action the monkey's motor neuron activated again and again while simply watching the researcher. These neurons were subsequently named mirror neurons. Neurons that activate while watching somebody else move—mirroring their actions in our own brains (Rizzolatti et al. 1996).

The paper Rizzolatti wrote was initially rejected by the journal it was submitted to for its lack of general interest. However, it was shortly after almost euphorically received and this has led to an impetus of research into mirror neurons in primates and humans. Indeed they are considered essential elements of our social brain, our ability to connect to others and are implied in fields such as learning by imitation,

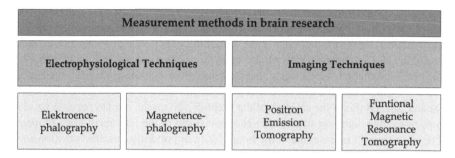

Fig. 2.9 Methods of brain research

empathy and even the building of civilisation (Ramachandran 2000). Many highly respected neuroscientists have drawn our attention to their value. Autism has, for example, been implicated in dysfunction of the mirror neuron system (Williams et al. 2001).

Mirror neurons can activate to actions, emotions but also intentions. This shows that we are connected to the world around us and we live a little bit of the actions but also the emotions and intentions we perceive (Rizzolatti and Fabbri-Destro 2010). This is the value of the social brain: we *are* connected to the environment and the people around us.

The strength of the mirroring is however, affected by various factors:

- The emotional development in childhood affects significantly ability to be able to connect and empathise (Gordon 2003).
- Mirroring is stronger when it is directly linked with satisfying a particular need.
- Mirroring works best when the observer can understand and is familiar with the context of the observations.

Different areas of mirror neurons have now been mapped and these cover large regions of the cerebral cortex and especially the motor regions. In a simplified understanding these are the neurons that help us connect to each other including inter-brain synchronization during social interaction (Dumas et al. 2010).

2.6   Methods of Brain Research

The current methods of research are responsible for the amount of knowledge we have about the brain: it is also the development in the technology that we have to thank for the information that we have. It is after all the advances in these areas that have driven the depth and clarity of knowledge. Though there are a wide variety of techniques now available we will look at the most common which account for the vast majority of research. We can put the techniques into two categories (see Fig. 2.9). Firstly techniques that measure electrical activity in the brain: electroencephalography (EEG) and magnetoencephalography (MEG). These measure the minute electrical impulses in various regions and operate in real time. These show us the immediate electrical reactions in the brain in certain regions in the cerebral cortex. Secondly the ways of imaging the brain, techniques that can give pictures of

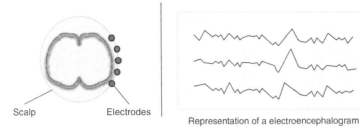

Scalp   Electrodes
                              Representation of a electroencephalogram

Fig. 2.10 Electroencephalography

the brain and its workings. These techniques measure the increase of activity in various regions of the brain. The measurement is based on various criteria such as increased oxygen use in these areas or transfer of water molecules. These give the very popular coloured 3-D diagrams showing the precise regions activated, importantly also deep in the brain (Matthews and Jezzard 2004).

2.6.1   Electroencephalography

Electroencephalography (Davidson et al. 2000) is one of the oldest techniques in neuroscience research. You will be familiar with the pictures of people sitting with electrodes over various parts of the head. It origins go back to the 1920s. In today's scientific environment it is now seldom used independently but still has the advantage that the readings are real time in microsecond intervals which is an advantage over the imaging techniques which are only taken in intervals of a few seconds. As we know the brain communicates at microsecond intervals and so this can show immediate reactions to a stimuli. In addition it is a cheap technique, it is transportable and can be used in a variety of contexts. More than that it enables the researched person to be able to move to a limited extent or sit at a computer for example which is not possible, or difficult, with other techniques. Currently there are now various simplified EEG models on the market used for techniques such as neurofeedback and in some cases simple popular brain programmes.

The electrodes are fastened to the head (or a cap is used) and these pick up the fluctuations in the electrical patterns. As we know neurons communicate with small electrical impulses (known as action potentials) that are generated by differences in the so-called ion channels. These minute electrical impulses can, when regions of neurons activate, generate an electrical current that can be measured on the scalp (Fig. 2.10).

2.6.2   Magnetoencephalography

Magnetoencephalography (Ioannides 2009) is a development of EEG and was developed at the start of the 1990s. This technique measures the magnetic fields

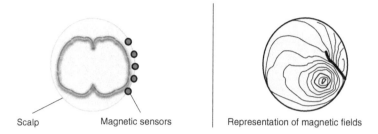

Fig. 2.11 Magnetoencephalography

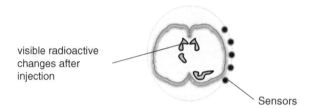

Fig. 2.12 Positron emission tomography

produced by the brain. This give a magnetic field picture of the brain and it fluctuations and changes but its advantage over EEG is that it can also show activity in the deeper brain regions and not just in the outer layers of the cerebral cortex (Fig. 2.11).

2.6.3 Positron Emission Tomography (PET)

Positron Emission Tomography (developed around 1974) measures the radioactivity in glucose after the candidate has been injected with a radioactive glucose liquid (see Fig. 2.12) (Casse et al. 2004).

This weakly radioactive substance can be taken up by the brain and it shows the regions that are using higher levels of glucose (the brain's energy source) and hence pointing to the regions that are most active. This activity can then be mapped onto 3-D model of the brain and we can therefore see models of the regions that are activating and not activated to given stimuli. The images given here, though using different techniques, are similar to those produced by Magnetic Resonance Imaging (MRI).

2.6.4 Functional Magnetic Resonance Imaging (fMRI)

Functional Magnetic Resonance Imaging (Matthews and Jezzard 2004) is very common in research because of the widespread availability of the machines, despite

Fig. 2.13 fMRI images

their cost. The machines are so widespread because of the value of their abilities. Magnetic Resonance Imaging measures the movement and magnetization of molecules in the body. These can give clear 3-D pictures of the whole body in detailed clarity and minute detail of internal organs. Magnetic resonance imaging as a technique, in spite of it's value in detecting brain tumours, for example, is of little value in functional and cognitive fields because a picture takes minutes and only represents the structure and not the function. The functional technique therefore uses information gleaned from the haemoglobin molecules (relating to blood supply) and can in much quicker snapshots measure the change in oxygen usage in different parts of the brain. These snaps are in time frames of around 3 s. These are then plotted onto 3-D maps of the brain showing close to real time activation of various areas of the brain—as neurons activate so do their oxygen consumption. The pictures represent the areas of oxygen usage in different parts of the brain and the subsequent images are in 2-D or 3-D (see Fig. 2.13). The images it should be noted do not directly measure the neuronal activity but that of oxygen usage.

2.6.5   Diffusion Tensor Imaging (DTI)

Diffusion Tensor Imaging (Tournier et al. 2011) is an MRI technique. This has only recently been refined to a level that it is increasingly being used in neuroscientific research. It has its roots in the work of Michael Moseley in the early 1990s who reported on the water molecule movement in white matter (the myleniated axons connecting the cerebral cortex to other areas in the brain). This has since 1995 been increasingly used in research. Its real value lies in being able to detect the pathways and connections in the brain. From these multitude of regions in the brain not all are connected to each other and to be able to observe these connections, the paths and highways between regions, is increasing our understanding of how parts of the brain communicate to each other.

2.6.6   The State of Play on Technology

The above are the most commonly used techniques. There are, however, others: Computed Axial Tomography (CAT), Single Photon Emission Computed Tomography (SPECT) to name some common abbreviations in neuroscience. However these are falling into the background particularly those that require injection of radioactive fluid (as the above do) as this is an invasive technology and limits the amount of research that can be carried out on any one individual. So all forms of MRI are the preferred technique, this in itself is becoming ever more refined with techniques such as diffusion tensor imaging but also ever increasing ability to obtain readings at smaller intervals moving closer to real time measuring of the brain's activity.

EEG is used relatively seldom nowadays as an independent technique but is still often seen used in conjunction with other techniques to gain insights into real time activation. It has reached a new niche in neurofeedback which can be used successfully in some serious dysfunctions such as autism but also in popularised cases of sports psychology, in anger management but also in brain computer interface "games" claiming benefits of the brain. However here also further technical developments are showing better levels of reading at deeper levels in the brain.

Further research is also looking in to the gene activation in the brain. The Allen Institute for Brain Research (set up by Microsoft founder Paul Allen) has recently completed a full genetic mapping of the brain in mice (Lerch et al. 2009) and humans (Holmes 2011) including also a mapping of genetic expression during development (in the mouse brain) (The Allen Brain Atlas can be visited and searched online at: http://www.brain-map.org). These are exciting discoveries but with less immediate impact for neuroleadership: Genetic expression will show how different neurons express themselves and how they react to various neurotransmitters and hence is incredibly important for looking into various neurological disorders.

In research two other areas of knowledge are also tapped into. The first, and the oldest methodology apart from dissection of the brain is that of tumour research. When we know a patient has a tumour or lesion in a part of the brain, we can see what changes occur in this patient's behaviour. Much early work was based on this. The famous case of Broca's area (speech production) and Wernicke's area (language comprehension) were discovered based on tumours in patients and these descriptions of the changes in behaviour that occurs as a follow on from this—in these particular cases aphasia, the loss of parts of language.

In research Transcranial Magnetic Stimulation (TMS) (Kobayashi and Pascual-Leone 2003) is a technique commonly used. This technique activates various parts of the brain through light magnetic signals from electrodes placed on the scalp. This means that an area of the brain can be activated or inhibited. The electrical signals will disturb the electrical function of the neurons in that region and so scientists can "shut down" a region and then research the effects of this (or increase the stimulation depending on the frequency used).

As we write this in 2012 we are in an exciting time as the technology is ever improving and we are seeing better and better imaging techniques. Diffusion Tensor Imaging shows a powerful part of the picture, as the connections are essential to understanding the brain's functions. The increased speed of fMRI is also giving us a more realistic picture of the brain. Though we are a long, long way from being able to mind read, to read thoughts and intentions from the scans, these techniques are ever more being used in criminal cases. In September 2011 Professor Jack Gallant at UC Berkeley released a report documenting the reconstruction of images being viewed on video (Nishimoto et al. 2011). Though crude the computer reconstructions from the brain imaging were at times clearly identifiable.

The research into gene expression will likely be fundamental in finding deeper clues to neurological disorders. We expect the technology to continue advancing and to have ever more refined view of the brain in all fields of research.

We will now look deeper into the actual results of this research and into the brain and particularly that of emotions.

2.7   The Impact of Emotions on Neural Processes

When we speak of emotions scientists are all aware of their impact on the human being, indeed emotions are an integral part of being human and our consequent actions and reactions. Our language also reflects this importance with a huge amount of descriptive terms for emotion of all colours and forms. Yet, this said, there is no definitive taxonomy of emotions and no generally accepted method of classification. We will, therefore, look into what we mean by emotions and define the terms of affect, mood, feeling and emotion (Schönpflug 2000).

Affect is the experience of feeling or emotions and represents a response to stimuli. We use it here to refer to it as a response that will have some form of emotional or physical manifestation whether consciously processed or not. These can also be the less consciously processed emotions which will affect the mood of the employee in the workplace without having significant emotional impact. These affects are important parts of the workplace as many may be instinctive and short lived but contribute to the whole experience of an emotion and its physical manifestation but also of the behavioural manifestation. If an emotion is affective it will drive to action.

Moods are representations of broad emotions in a form that influences an individual over time and colours the way we see the world during that mood. Many people will speak of being in a good mood or a bad mood and we have many words to describe these. We can see moods as the spectacles though which we are currently seeing the world but these will also have significant impacts on motivation and interpersonal interactions in the workplace. An event which triggers a strong emotion can give rise to a mood. Yet many moods have no clear conscious trigger. In this sense also moods are the mix of emotions that we are experiencing that will then produce a broader emotion represented as a mood. Notably these can also have positive or negative knock on effects and this is particularly significant in the work place. Fiedler noted that people who are positive and optimistic are more trusting and place more trust in their environment, master problems better and develop creative solutions quicker (Fiedler 1988). People who are more negative look more for safety, are afraid to make mistakes and are often tense. Interestingly moods in the workplace are rarely measured. With the exception of the usual employee satisfaction surveys there seems to be no interest or way to measure the moods of the workforce and little effort is being made to approach this. Yet it is likely that precisely these moods are having subtle and powerful effects on the way the work is being carried out.

Feeling is a term which is often used interchangeably with emotions. The etymology shows us clearly what drives the meaning here. Feeling, from the stem feel, is the physical representation of an object e.g. of warmth. Thus feelings are classed as the conscious subjective experience of emotion. Feeling is the affect of emotion. This is the physical manifestation and representation of an emotion and not the emotion itself. "I feel warm inside" may represent the emotion of love but also of friendship of gratitude and many more. Feelings are the body's internal communication system of emotion and are also driven strongly by the hormones and chemicals in the brain (see Sect. 2.9.1).

Emotions are the psychophysiological state of mind from the interaction of internal and external processes. These are conscious manifestations that will colour our feelings and internal representation and affect our subsequent mood. There are a wide variety of emotions we can experience which we can see as scales on a rainbow with various emotions colouring others and these can be experienced with a variety of intensities. Think of the word happy: elated, joyous, satisfied, are all variations of this. Some people separate basic emotions and complex emotions. The basic emotions working somewhat like the primary colours and the complex emotions are variations and mixes of these. Paul Ekman the world's leading expert on facial expression categorised six basic emotions in the 1970s: anger disgust, fear, happiness, sadness, surprise (Ekman et al. 1982). He expanded this list in the 1990s to include: amusement, contempt, contentment, embarrassment, excitement, guilt, pride in achievement, relief, satisfaction, sensory pleasure, shame.

Emotions are particularly relevant for corporations because these will affect the mood. But more specifically if we are talking about the brain-directed man, we know that emotions come in combination with chemical processes in the brain and body and these will have an affective impact meaning increased energy increased, or decreased motivation, increased focus, etc. Furthermore we also know from the research into mirror neurons that emotions are also mirrored and hence to no small extent infectious. Emotions of individuals and of the mass will be directly impacting the mood in any business and on the general atmosphere and in turn the chemical balance in the brain and body and in turn ability to operate optimally in any given context.

2.7.1 Emotional Intelligence

In parallel to the increased understanding of emotions and their fundamental importance in the brain the concept of emotional intelligence has also developed. Emotional intelligence was first proposed, in some form, in 1983 as a result of Howard Gardener's work into multiple intelligences whereby he defined intrapersonal and interpersonal intelligence as one of eight "intelligences" (Gardner 1983). Emotional intelligence became a mainstream movement in the 1990s with Daniel Goleman taking a leading role in its conceptualization (Goleman et al. 2001). We now have a more refined understanding of what emotional intelligence constitutes. Daniel Goleman defines five competencies on the two axis of Intrapersonal and Interpersonal Competencies (Fig. 2.14).

Dimensions of emotional intelligence	
Intrapersonal competencies	Interpersonal competencies
Self-awareness	Social awareness
Self-regulation	Social competence
Self-motivation	

Fig. 2.14   Dimensions of emotional intelligence

Self-awareness is the ability to be able to introspect and to be aware of one's own feelings and motives and also one's own effect on others. It includes being able to identify one's own moods, feelings and motivations, to understand how we respond to various external, or internal, stimuli. But also to understand one's effect on other people, how other people react to ourselves, our actions and comments.

To be able to control one's own mood and be minimally affected by external stimuli. To have an own mood which is not affected by external input. A person with high self control will not jump to impulsive decisions but will think clearly and make well-thought out and controlled decisions.

According to Goleman if you have **self-motivation** you will, and can work on problems and projects without an external extrinsic reward such as money or status. These people can follow, with energy, zeal and commitment, a goal to its completion for the sake of its completion and nothing more. Commitment and optimism will help overcome any hurdles and setbacks.

Under **social awareness** empathy plays a leading role: the ability to put oneself in another's position and share their emotions and standpoint without getting pulled under by these emotions or perceptions. In this sense empathy increases our ability to understand other people and also understand their motives and drives to a deeper and more fundamental level. Generally this also goes hand in hand with a clear understanding of one's own emotions. Furthermore social awareness includes the whole set of competencies that is needed to read emotions and the impact of these on others in social contexts.

Social competence is the ability to adapt to social situations and configurations and in these varying contexts to be able to inspire and influence through effective communication skills and in addition the ability to relate and tap into other's emotions and motives. It is also about collaboration and ability to build relationships and build bonds with others and includes, amongst others, conflict management and the ability to leave people feeling valued.

We approach emotional leadership in the context of neuroleadership and the four basic human needs in Sect. 5.4.4.

2.7.2   Neuroscientific Aspects of Stress and Fear

We would now like to look into specifics of emotions to illustrate the importance of these to the body and illustrate the underlying processes. These, we feel are essential to understand in the context of neuroleadership. We will specifically

| Amygdala | Hypothalamus | Pituitary gland | Adrenal gland | Blood stream |

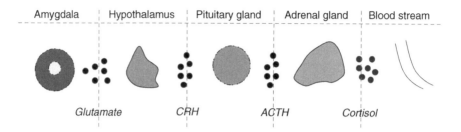

Glutamate   CRH   ACTH   Cortisol

Fig. 2.15 HTPA-Axis

look into one of the most important stress responses: the HTPA-Axis (hypothalamic-pituitary-adrenal axis) (Swaab et al. 2005). This axis we use not to demonstrate the complexity of the chemical and hormonal processes but to understand the connections that the brain has with the body and the immediate short-term and long–term impact this can have on the human being in or out of corporations. The specific terminology is therefore less relevant for us but we would like you to understand the powerful connections and principles that drive this. Figure 2.15 is a diagrammatic representation of the HTPA-Axis.

Fear activates the amygdala in the brain which in turn will, through release of the transmitter glutamate, activate other regions in the brain stem and hypothalamus. This kicks off the stress-response cascade. The hypothalamus releases CRH (corticotropin-releasing hormone) which in turn signals to the pituitary gland to release adrenocorticotropic hormone which is sent into the bloodstream stream and then circulates to the adrenal gland where it binds and then stimulates the final step in the cascade, the release of cortisol into the bloodstream which has a widespread impact on the system.

Cortisol functions in many ways but helps the body fight the stress by releasing and redistributing energy to critical parts of the body e.g. the heart and away from non-critical parts of the body (in the short-term) e.g. the digestive system. Importantly it will also immediately take away resources from the body's immune system. These are in the short-term and for short-term stress reactions of little consequence to the body. It is after all a natural system of defence and a natural reaction and serves a purpose. However chronic stress over lengthy periods, as we can understand with the above description, will have a significant impact on the system and can be a cause of increased sickness and deterioration in health in addition to a whole host of others symptoms in various parts of the body.

Fear however, is processed differently by different people: from one's own perception of what fear is but also there has recently been a so-called anti-stress gene identified that controls and regulates CRH production and its over or under production (Amir-Zilberstein et al. 2012).

However the real danger of fear lies in its physical representation in hormones and chemicals in the body which imbalance the system. Furthermore these can then become associated to various stimuli and become conditioned into the brain and the body.

Leading by using fear, we can see in this short section, is for certain going to lead to a host of negative effects and impacts on human beings. The misconception that "fear can motivate" lies not in the fact that fear is a motivator but that fear can get to action, particularly in absence of any other ability to "motivate" (Nakatani et al. 2009). The host of negative impacts should lead us to use other more positive motivational drivers which will lead to healthier corporations. Obviously the reward system here is a better motivator and, indeed, dopamine is a powerful counter chemical to stress. Simply by showing interest in a person and being friendly and helpful has been shown to reduce fear and subsequent stress.

We will now look into the brain to see what distortions fear has on the brain's regional functioning. This will highlight the importance of fear and what a powerful force it is in distorting and manipulating the brain, drawing it into a negative spiral which will cause all sorts of disruptions in the brain and indeed even inhibit higher cognitive abilities.

2.7.2.1 Functional Impact of Fear in the Brain

Fear as outlined above has a significant negative impact on the hormonal balance in the brain and in the body. This can, in extreme cases, particularly with long-term fear, anxiety or stress, lead to conditions such as burnout. However looking into the regional activation in the brain paints a worrying picture of specific regional brain inhibition and activation which is also a cause of concern for businesses. Indeed even at a macro economic level this has a significant impact.

As we know the amygdala is directly connected to the prefrontal cortex, the frontal lobes of the brain, where many of our executive functions sit. This includes regions that balance emotions in the orbital frontal cortex in advance of making decisions. What research has also shown is that the prefrontal cortex can also exert control over the amygdala (Dolan 2007). This connection is a two-way street. This is encouraging as it means we can control our emotions to a degree. However, this connection is problematic in that we know that an overactive amygdala can inhibit functioning in the prefrontal cortex. This includes a region called the dorsolateral prefrontal cortex. This region specifically is also responsible for short-term memory (Petrides 2000). What this means is that, in short, an overactive amygdala will inhibit rational thinking and information balancing in the prefrontal cortex but also reduces our short-term memory leading to a decreased ability to deal with complexity. Short-term memory and fluid intelligence seem tightly linked together and our ability to keep things in our mind so that we can balance and compare them (Shelton et al. 2010). In summary fear decreases, cognitive ability—our ability to process complexity. Fear, in short, makes us stupid.

A study by Feinstein et al. (2010) documented the case of SM a woman who has a rare condition called Urbach–Wiethe disease, which has destroyed here amygdalae. Her response to typical fearful situations was non-existent. Horror films amused her, she said she didn't like snakes but had not fear of them. She lives in a poverty stricken area and her life has been threatened on two occasions but she displayed no fear or urgency in theses situations (but did feel anger).

A further impact of an active amygdala is that it will activate the fight or flight response system and this means an increase in energy. The fight or flight response, as the name implies, means that the body will put itself in a position to fight, with increased energy and aggressiveness, or flee with increased energy (more correctly it should be the "freeze, fight, flight or fright" response) (Bracha et al. 2004). Both will also lead to a focusing of, a narrowing of, vision onto the single point of danger. This excess energy can lead to increased action in combination with aggressive protective behaviour. This will counteract any collaborative activities. The urge to flee will manifest itself in the workplace with individuals ignoring, or not tackling, current problems and issues, running away from them so to speak. A further effect is the freeze response when the motor cortex is effectively shut down. The freeze reflex will manifest itself in an inability to act in business scenarios, including an inability to make decisions. These fear reactions are significant for corporations as this means either thoughtless action or inaction both of which have the ability to severely negatively impact any corporation.

In addition to this, research has shown that what we normally implicitly feel, is indeed supported by science, namely that our perceptions and bias changes. We shift our bias to negativity (Sharot et al. 2007). In a previous example we used the analogy of seeing a coiled rope lying on the ground and immediately mistaking it for a snake. Negative bias means that even though we realised it was not a snake, our sensitivity to snakes will have *increased*. If it were a snake we would assuming we escaped this one safely, which is statistically very probable, increase our focus and be increasingly sensitive to snake-like shapes in the surroundings. Specifically in the brain the anterior cingulate cortex (ACC) sitting above the limbic system, as we have noted, is a structure that, amongst others, helps focus our attention and monitor the environment for discrepancies. This area becomes active and will increase its negative bias now finding more and more snake-like shapes in the environment. The immediate effect of this in a businesses context is that in times of fear the negativity will increase and the chances of finding negative information also (Whalen et al. 2001). This can in turn influence the whole mood of an organisation. Furthermore this is also important and observable at a macroeconomic level. It will also explain how the popular press works as, for example, recession looms, fear will seep through society and our sensitivity and attraction to further negative events increases. The newspapers will slowly fill with negative stories and we will be drawn along in an ever-increasing flood of information which will in turn continue to activate our fear centres (Fig. 2.16).

The reaction to fear itself is an impulsive survival instinct and important to us— yet the danger this poses to us in the field of neuroleadership is that we are no longer scanning the environment while roaming through the undergrowth of the countryside, we are operating in corporations and need to deal with complexity and need our cognitive powers to work creatively and efficiently and moreover to operate collaboratively. Fear will counteract this ability and give rise to focused aggressive behaviour, with an inability to deal with complexity, reduced cognitive powers and a host of hormonal imbalances.

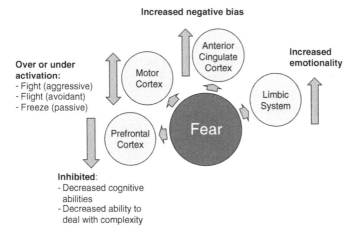

Fig. 2.16 Functional impact of fear in the brain

2.7.2.2 The Power of Faces and Unconscious Fear

In Sect. 2.5.3 we noted how mirror neurons link us to the actions of others. This is also reflected in the brain's reaction to faces. Specifically research into our reactions of fearful faces shave shown that just by looking at fearful faces this will stimulate our amygdala, stimulate fear that is (Whalen et al. 1998). This demonstrates how connected we are to our to the environment around us and particularly the people around us. This is also very relevant for corporate environments and the emotions that are demonstrated and expressed, openly or not, in corporations. Corporations are after all groups of people whose emotions will be influencing each other.

The more interesting research, though, is that of a similar set of experiments, as in the above studies. Specifically looking into our reaction to masked, subliminally presented that is, faces. In masking techniques a series of pictures will be shown and between these, other "masked" images will be inserted. These are masked by exposing these at an exposure time of less than 30 ms. Below 30 ms we do not consciously process visual stimuli but only unconsciously. If exposed below 10 ms no response conscious or unconscious can be seen. When fearful faces were masked, inserted that is, between normal images at exposures of less than 30 ms, the amygdala also activated even though the subjects had no conscious knowledge that they had seen fearful faces (Whalen et al. 1998). This shows that fear can be processed unconsciously *without* our explicit knowledge. This is also very relevant for corporations because in fearful environments we may not even be conscious that fear has activated and the functional differences we noted above may be distorting our thinking processes.

2.7.3   Functional Effects of Emotions in Organisations

Subjective and interpersonal emotions fulfil an important function in daily business (and yet are rarely mentioned in business literature). An emotional free business environment that many seem to have strived for, is not only unrealistic and a fallacy, it is nigh near an impossibility. Having emotions is what defines us as human beings and defines our sense of self. Emotions also have various clear functions in organisational contexts (Küpers and Weibler 2005):

- Signal function
- Decision supporting function
- Behavioural function
- Cohesive function.

1. **Signal function**

   Emotions are expressed in different ways and manners. More than that, emotions are expressive tools and therefore a powerful communication tool. Understanding emotions can in this sense function as a signal to tell the organisation of information in the system. It has a feedback function but also potentially has a warning function. Understanding emotions will allow management to better tap into their employees and communicate at the same level and so increase the efficiency of an organisation.

2. **Decision supporting function**

   As we previously saw (see Sect. 2.6.2) our rational centres in the prefrontal cortex are directly linked to our emotional centres. Our orbitofrontal cortex is a great balancer of information and this information is processed consciously and unconsciously. By tying our emotions into decisions we are using more brain resources and using the power of a subconscious that can tap into much more information than the conscious can. When we talk of using emotions we do not mean being emotional i.e. using excessive emotions such as anger, fear or elation to make decisions—this is a recipe for disaster. Rather we mean use good common sense listen to your "gut"[6] and make well-balanced decisions.

3. **Behavioural function**

   Emotions affect the behaviours of employees. Either through their speed and efficiency but also through a mental preparation process whereby the work can be cognitively worked through and hence efficiency increased. As we have seen, emotions affect the hormonal balance in the brain and in the body and these will put the mind and body in an optimal state for whatever type of work lies ahead. In service industries the ability to deal with complexity may be in the forefront and in industrial contexts the ability to work efficiently but also to pre-empt any problems or disruptions will help improve working processes.

4. **Cohesive function**

   Emotion promotes in different ways the cohesion of a work force. The simple bonding and trust that is placed in each other and in leadership and vice versa. A longitudinal study in 2008 (Salamon and Robinson 2008) in the USA noted a

---

[6] There have been a number of books that have focused on gut feeling in recent years, the most popular being "Blink" by Malcolm Gladwell, 2005.

correlation between trusting workplaces[7] and productivity. Trust is in itself a key element of bonding. This will also help to reduce conflict, increase the level of communication and simply make the workplace a much more pleasant place to be. This in turn will affect and limit the stressors in the workplace and enable more people to work to their potential making work in general a more enjoyable experience. All workplaces rely on collaboration of some sort and the bigger corporations ever more so—these are driven by and need to have various components such as emotional bonding to make this a more efficient system. See also basic needs discussion in Chap. 4 and particularly attachment in Sect. 4.2.1.

In addition it should be noted that emotions and hormonal balances are also the key components of disorders and illness in many forms. Making the workplace healthier from the brain's perspective can only produce better results for the organisation and much of this is driven though the emotional systems in the brain. Organisations themselves can also increase the emotional bonding in various ways:

- **Rationalisation:** in being able to identify with the rationally formulated goals of an organisation we can stem irrational fears.
- **Projection:** fears and energy can be focused externally to competitors and markets.
- **Regression:** in the organisational network of organisations various hierarchical needs can be respected and rewarded.
- **Sublimation:** organisations provide a place to live out various energies that cannot be fulfilled in other contexts e.g. competitive instincts (towards competitors) which may cause conflict in family situations or in social circles.

2.8   The Power of the Limbic System

Neuroscientists have come to see the concept of free will in a different light. The whole concept of free will in itself has been questioned by Stephen Hawking (Hawking and Mlodinov 2010) amongst many others and what is certain is that a lot of free will is an illusion. This does not mean that we do not decide but rather that our decision making draws on underlying schemata we have laid down over the years an these unconscious processes colour and influence all our decisions. We know that rationalisation is often only a cover for our decisions.[8] Indeed that decisions are made in the brain before we consciously believe we have made a decision, on making a decision we then post-rationalise our decision. The limbic

---

[7] A more worrying side in corporate contexts is that the Harvard Business Review reported in 2006 that roughly half of managers do not trust their leaders—and 80 % of Americans do not trust corporate executives.

[8] There has been a lot of work on rationalisation starting as far back as 1931 with Norman F. Meier's now legendary rope trick. Nisbett's 1977 paper "Telling more than we can know: Verbal reports on mental processes" was a landmark paper and is still informative more than 40 years after being written.

system is responsible for this process—the emotional anchoring of processes and patterns that we draw on in the quick decision-making circuits that are all processed unconsciously.

Many scientists will argue that we may not have a free will but we have a "free won't" and indeed we know that the cerebral cortex can influence the limbic system. The pathway is a two-way street. However this is significant for us in neuroleadership as we know that under stress and in fearful situations the functioning of the higher executive areas of our brain in the prefrontal cortex are suppressed and that we have therefore less of an ability to influence our limbic system and we then go back to our underlying decision-making processes and often our primitive survival reactions.

The dominance of the limbic system in our thought processes and decision-making ability is of key importance for organisations for if we want employees to learn new skills and behave in different ways we will need to reprogramme the limbic system and this is not an overnight process. Change is not a quick process but a consistent and focused process designed to change the underlying processing of the limbic system. We do know that everyone can learn, as the insights in neuroplasticity show, but we also have to understand how this functions and this functions with the limbic system and especially the reward system.

2.9   Neurochemical Processes

So far we have looked at the regions in the brain and some of their manifestations in function. Yet all of these processes are driven by the biological communication of neurons. This biological interaction is driven by chemical processes that are released between and in neurons. We therefore would like to briefly look at the chemicals in the brain.

Chemical transmitters in the brain are released in different regions and in different situations leading to and generating different feelings. We have already mentioned various hormones and transmitters such as dopamine in reward and attention and CHR at the start of the stress cascade. The feelings we perceive and feel are not merely brain functions but are primarily dependant on the excretion of certain chemicals and hormones in the brain and in the body in general. These transmitters in the brain have various functions, they can be inhibitory i.e. they inhibit the functioning of neurons or they can be excitatory i.e. excite and stimulate the function of neurons. As each cell has different receptors there can be different receptors for each chemical—this means that, for example dopamine can dock into four different types of receptor depending on the neuron and these have different functions, inhibitory or excitatory. It is therefore important to have a brief overview of some of the key chemicals in the brain and also a brief look into cognitive enhancement which has received increasing media attention in recent years.

2.9.1 Neurotransmitters and their Functions

The brain is a biological electrical circuit of incredible complexity and this circuit is driven by biological electrical processes which are stimulated by a host of different chemical substances. We will look at the four key transmitters in the brain that influence broad circuits and key functions. These are: acetylcholine, serotonin, dopamine und noradrenaline. These transmitters work in large networks of neurons and regions.

The **acetylcholine** system influences memory formation and is therefore important in memory performance. It also plays a role in sustaining attention (Perry et al. 1999).

The **serotonin** system plays a key role in mood particularly in fear and aggression (Duman and Canli 2010). Serotonin is also produced in the gut (90 % is actually produced in the digestive tracts) and thus it also gauges food availability (and is thus responsible for irritability and anger of, particularly, men when hungry). It has other wide reaching effects varying from influencing cardiovascular health to gauge of social situations, mating behaviours and gauges of social status.

The **dopamine** system is an extensive network that influences key areas in the brain and generates key feelings such as euphoria (see Sect. 2.5.2). The dopamine system runs from the limbic system to the prefrontal areas of the brain where our executive functions sit. It is therefore an important element of attention and ADHD is thought to have its roots in a lack of dopamine. Many ADHD drugs are dopamine supplements or boosters (such as Ritalin—see Sect. 2.9.2). In general it also serves as our reward drug inducing feelings of happiness and euphoria. On the negative side it also plays a role in compulsion (Van Winkle 2000). In combination with oxytocin it produces powerful bonding feelings.

Noradrenaline (or norepinephrine) is produced from dopamine and is responsible for the fight or flight response (Gerson et al. 2009) and its affects include increased heart rate, increased oxygen supply to the brain and muscles and release of glucose into the blood stream. It is therefore a key stress response chemical. It also plays a role in attention particularly with reference to realistic shift prediction (Van Winkle 2000; Corbetta and Shulman 2002; Devauges and Sara 1990). As with dopamine, lowered levels of this are implicated in ADHD.

There are currently over 50 substances that we know of that operate as transmitters in the brain. Drugs and medication can magnify, decrease or inhibit their influences. Here is a short list of transmitters and their actions (Table 2.1).

It is important to note that though these have been well researched in part, that the imaging technologies that we discussed in Sect. 2.5 show brain activation but do not give deeper clues to the actual chemical transmissions in these regions. For this there is much research done with animals to give us deeper clues as to how the various systems work.

2.9.2 Cognitive Enhancement

Casually known as "brain doping", cognitive enhancement (technically nootropics) aims to improve the functioning of the brain particularly in the context of attention,

Table 2.1 Selected neurotransmitters (Based on Seidel 2004, p 132)

Neurotransmitter	Influence
Acetylcholine	Memory, attention
Serotonin	Fear, decision-making, mood
Noradrenaline	Energy, mood, attention
Dopamine	Feelings of reward, attention
Endomorphin (or Endorphin)	Well being
Oxytocin	Trust, love
Corticosteroids	Stress, anger
GABA-deficiency	Fear disorders
Testosterone	Dominance, aggression

energy and memory consolidation through taking specific chemical supplements and/or medication (Auf dem Hövel 2008).

The use of such cognitive enhancers has drastically increased in recent years. In 2007 a study (Sahakian and Morein-Zamir 2007) noted that 7 % of students at college (in the USA) had used cognitive enhancers to achieve an edge in the year preceding the study and on some campuses the figure was as high as 25 %. According to a study in Germany in 2009 (Krämer and Nolting 2009) over two million people have already tried such drugs and 800,000 use them regularly. There has also been much publicity in the press. For example the *New Yorker* ran an article in 2009 (Talbot 2009) focusing on undergraduates and academics at universities. Further articles have appeared in the *New York Times* and *Time* to name but a few.

These cognitive enhancers unlike the classic boosters coffee and tobacco, specifically target various transmitters and hence brain regions and specific effects such as increased attention. Many of these drugs were originally developed to treat sicknesses such as Alzheimer's and ADHD and are now seen as tools to increase performance (Table 2.2).

The above are some very specific enhancers and there are however a whole host of others that have their roots in dietary supplementation and sports performance, NAC, alpha GPC but also creatine and L-carnitine have well documented research showing their impacts in the brain (Rae et al. 2003). For example, the amino acid L-Tyrosine is a precursor to dopamine and norepinephrine and hence can operate in a similar way to dopamine enhancers.

However there should be a healthy dose of scepticism here. In looking into the brain in neuroleadership our goal is to look into how the brain functions and how these can best function with this we include a healthy chemical environment in the brain. A healthy brain and a healthy environment indeed will produce a healthy chemical environment within our cranium. Using drugs to try to counteract an unhealthy environment is not a solid solution. Healthy food and healthy eating and sleeping habits will do more than any single chemical to balance the brain. Indeed in Sect. 2.9.1 we noted that 90 % of serotonin is produced in the gut and unhealthy eating habits will also influence the production of serotonin in the digestive tract. The brain derives its energy from glucose and the long-term release of good quality glucose will influence our brain functioning as will a ready supply of micro- and

Table 2.2 Popular cognitive enhancers

Methylphenidate	**Methylphenidate** is the key component of Ritalin that is used to treat ADHD. This is increasingly being used by students, scientists and managers to increase their ability to concentrate. Methylphenidate increases the levels of dopamine and noradrenalin in the brain through inhibition of the reuptake receptors and this can lead to improvement of mood (to euphoria) increased concentration and inhibition of hunger and drowsiness but with a potential loss of the sense of reality.
Donepezil	**Donepezil** is marketed as Aricept for the treatment of Alzheimer und dementia. Donepezil influences the function of the stimulatory paths of nerve cells and improves cognitive and memory processes.
Modafinil	In 2008 Provigil was re-classed in Germany as a prescription drug and no longer a controlled substance. In the USA, Canada, Australia and the UK is a prescription drug. **Modafinil** is licensed as a drug to treat narcolepsy, sleep disorders and daytime drowsiness. For this reason it is often used by students and managers. It was also thrown into the press spotlight with various sports doping cases. It was listed in 2004 as a prohibited substance by the World Anti-Doping Agency.
Adderall	Is a prescription drug only available in the USA and Canada but has had increasing press as a neuro enhancer. It is used against ADHD and narcolepsy. It operates by increasing the amount of dopamine and norepinephrine between synapses by inhibiting their reuptake in the brain.
Piracetam	Has widely reported cognitive benefits though rigorous scientific findings are still scarce. It increases oxygen consumption in the brain and ATP (cellular energy source) metabolism. It has been shown to improve cognition in dementia patients and other cases such as impairment from alcoholism and autism. It is widely available in the USA, Europe and other regions globally without prescription. Piracetam is part of the racetram group of substances— many used as cognitive enhancers.

macronutrients. Trying to redress the balance in the brain with some chemicals may be attractive but in the long run may be counterproductive particularly if the brain and body then come to rely on these.

However, this said, the rise of cognitive enhancement seems to be pre-programmed. After all with the demand of the workplace quick and easy fixes are certainly very attractive to many in the corporate environment if not to employers themselves. The increasing challenge in the modern workplace are also likely to drive more people to these enhancers.

Figures from the "DAK Health Study 2009"(DAK-Gesundheitsreport 2009)
43.5 % of the respondents know that taking drugs against age-influenced brain disorders, memory impairment and depression can also be effective for healthy people.

20.3 % of respondents stated that for healthy people the risk of taking these medications in relation to their benefits is acceptable.

21.4 % respondents said they had been recommended to take drugs to improve their cognitive abilities of their mood (the majority of these
(continued)

Fig. 2.17 Interaction between brain and environment

> *recommendations came from friends and relatives but also from the medical community).*
>
> *Experts rate the factors influencing the consumption of these drugs as, amongst others, increased time pressure, emotional work and competition in the workplace.*

2.10   A Brain-Friendly Environment

Given the information we have just covered we can see that there are a host of influencing factors that impact the brain. Indeed the environment and our interaction in this environment are constantly causing the brain and the neurons within this to fire in specific patterns. We therefore know that behaviour and experience forms the connections in the brain. We also have learnt that fear and negative emotions are bad from the standpoint of brain biology and that reward centre activation is positive. These are of crucial importance for us to understand as neuroleaders. They are crucial because little thought is given in business to a healthy brain environment—it is left to chance. And if the team interactions and the business environment happen to be positive so the impact on the brain will also be positive. Yet this can also change, by chance. The business environment can change, market conditions can change, new competitors can come into the market, team members can and do change as do members of the leadership team. These can then destabilise the context in which these brains are functioning and what was previously, by chance, a healthy brain environment will slip into a negative brain environment. The stakes are even higher than that because when times are tough that is precisely the moment that we need our brains to be operating at their optimum. Leaders often grapple in the dark here for solutions or switch to bad habits which can lead to a negative reinforcement cycles and lead to badly functioning brains but also physical stress, and in cases, severe clinical stress. This is bad for any business and costly too in terms of revenue lost, productivity lost let alone the personal human cost.

The knowledge we give here and specifically in Chaps. 4 and 5 are designed to enable you to create environments that are healthy for brains in business with all the positive consequences of this. The positive consequences are brains that can operate at their maximum ability: to be productive, creative, intelligent, reactive, flexible and open to change. This interaction between the environment, though, is continual.

The environment affects the people in the environment, and the people in the environment help to form the environment. The interaction in the environment creates the atmosphere and moods in the context and the perceptions of individuals may lead to different interpretations and hence also have an influence on the environment. Everything is connected to everything. It is a continual exchange back and forth. With time this will also rewire the brain in specific ways (see Fig. 2.17) we will approach this in more detail in Chaps. 4 and 5 after we have looked at some of the other key protagonists in the field of neuroleadership.

2.11 Summary

- **Neuroscience** includes a wide variety of disciplines that study the nervous system in general and specifically the brain including, amongst others:
  - **Neurobiology:** study of the structures, functions and development of nerve cells and the nervous system.
  - **Neurochemistry:** study of the chemical processes in the nervous system.
- The **brain** can be split into **three regions**:
  - **Brain stem:** instinctive reactions, reflexes and homeostasis
  - **Limbic system:** emotional centre
  - **Cerebrum:** higher forms of information processing
- Brain cells, **neurons**, consist of a cell body, axon and numerous dendrites
- **Plasticity** is the ability of the brain to keep building new connections (and hence continue learning)—this is possible for most of human life.
- The **reward system** is a system of structures in the limbic system that process reward and the feeling of happiness that this generates. These produce specifically the hormone dopamine that affects our feeling and also drives attention and learning.
- **Fear** stimulates the **amygdala** in the brain and also inhibits cognitive function and increases negative bias. Fight, flight and freeze are primitive instinctive dear reactions. The **HTPA axis** is a chemical stress cascade in the body.
- There are numerous methods of looking into and researching the brain. **fMRI** is the predominant method as it enables us to see what parts of the brain are activating and new methods are also enabling us to see the connections. This gives us concrete insights into the structural communication and functions of various regions.
- **Cognitive enhancement** is the targeted improvement of brain performance through drugs and supplements that are designed to increase, for example, attention, memory or energy.
- The brain can and does **change** but the environment must be suitable and the reward system needs to be activated.

Neuroscience in Business: Key Protagonists

3

The term "neuroleadership" is not new and neither is the idea of the brain driving human behaviour, interactions, personality and business interactions. This chapter therefore aims to summarise and outline some of the approaches that have been put forward over the years. We have chosen a number of protagonists who have specifically focused on the brain in business. We have not dealt with other names in the field, scientists and authors alike, that have focused on the brain in more general contexts as our purpose is to focus on the brain in specific business administration contexts.

Objectives

- Introduce five key figures using knowledge of neuroscience to define models for operating in business
- Understand the differences in their approaches
- Understand the similarities and how suitable their approaches are for implementation in business environments

3.1 Introduction

Neuroscience in leadership and corporate management is a recent development but there are a number of approaches in the market. Recent developments have led to a flood of literature on the topic of the brain with some focusing on business. Yet despite this flood of "neuro" topics there is still relative scarcity of solid literature scientifically backed up with direct applications to the corporate, organisational and leadership fields. This chapter therefore looks at some key figures in this area of literature and summarises their specific approaches.

We will look at the following figures:

- Ned Herrmann in his management career looked into how creativity developed and from this developed his Herrmann Brain Dominance Instrument which has become a popular tool for measuring personality types in corporations.

A. Ghadiri et al., *Neuroleadership*, Management for Professionals,
DOI 10.1007/978-3-642-30165-0_3, © Springer-Verlag Berlin Heidelberg 2012

- Gerald Hüther is a well-known name in the German speaking area; he is a respected neurobiologist and has published numerous popular books and articles on the brain and particularly with relevance to leadership and business administration.
- The only book with Neuroleadership in the title, until this one, was published by Christian E. Elger in 2009 in Germany. Elger, Director of the Department for Epistemology at the University Hospital in Bonn, is also another scientist who has focused intensively on the brain in corporate environments. He has also written on NeuroFinance and NeuroCommunication.
- David Rock coined the term neuroleadership with Jeffrey Schwartz of UCLA in 2006. He has written extensively on the brain in the workplace and founded the Neuroleadership Institute which pulls together scientists and personal development specialists alike.
- Srinivasan Pillay is one of the more recent additions to the field. Pillay has a background in psychology (Harvard Medical School) and neuroscience and has developed a detailed approach focused around leadership and coaching looking into the details of the brain's functioning.

3.2 Hermann's Brain Dominance Concept

The Herrmann Brain Dominance Instrument was inspired by the research in the 1970s particularly of brain lateralisation—notably by the work of Sperry and Gazzaniga (Sperry 1961; Gazzaniga 1998; Gazzaniga 2005). The test is a 120 item self-reporting questionnaire that can also be done online and places participants into four categories.

Herrmann's categorisation grew out of his work as a learning and education manager at GE and particularly his observation of personality types and the different ways that different people seemingly processed information. It was also around this time that the brain lateralisation concepts were being thrown into the public spotlight. Herrmann, through his study and observations, came to define four thinking modes based on a regional representation of the brain: left/right; up/down. See Fig. 3.1.

This model may seem very simplified and Herrmann did understand and also stress that there are many influences on the brain during growth: learning, upbringing, family, environment and so on and so forth and that each person will react to situations in a different way. Nevertheless he noted that according to research into brain lateralisation there exists certain dominance as to how and which parts of the brain we use.

It is now used and targeted at helping teams understand each other and to increase their productivity and creativity together. It is also seen as a personal developmental tool because if you can access more modes of thinking you will be able to access more knowledge and find more and better solutions.

The model has been criticised by some neuroscientists as oversimplified. This indeed does superficially seem to be the case yet brain lateralisation has been thrown into the spotlight again particularly by the masterful book by Iain McGilchrist "The Master and his Emissary" (McGilchrist 2009) which is a veritable

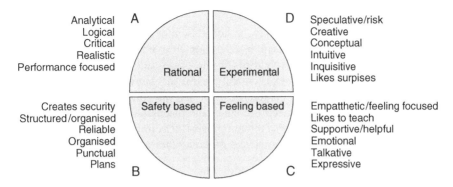

Analytical   A   D   Speculative/risk
Logical   Creative
Critical   Conceptual
Realistic   Intuitive
Performance focused   Rational   Experimental   Inquisitive
                                                                 Likes surpises

Creates security   Safety based   Feeling based   Empatthetic/feeling focused
Structured/organised   Likes to teach
Reliable   Supportive/helpful
Organised   Emotional
Punctual   Talkative
Plans   B   C   Expressive

Fig. 3.1 Herrmann's four modes of thinking (Hermann 1996, p 15)

Tour de Force scientifically documenting the lateralisation and specific functions of the hemispheres and their impact on our behaviours and interestingly, the whole evolution of modern man and modern society. Furthermore Coffield et al. (2004) in a systematic review of learning-style models reported favourably on Hermann's model—compared to the other 12 models that had managed to fulfil the criteria for being included in the study.

3.3 Supportive Leadership by Hüther

Hüther has written extensively (mostly in German) on what he has termed "Supportive Leadership". His writing approaches various organisational aspects that are necessary for a supportive working environment and also the qualities that a supportive leader should have. A supportive leader is one that develops the potential of their subordinates in place of using authority and repression (which will create a negative atmosphere of fear and uncertainty). In one of his articles "How brain friendly leadership works" he gives a set of rules for designing a suitable working environment (Hüther 2009). We have included Hüther because he gives concrete tips, guidelines and advice on how to create a neurobiologically suitable working environment. These according to Hüther are:

1. **Create new challenges**

   Management and leaders should ensure that employees can regularly take on new challenges. The brain gets used to, habituates to, routine tasks and is no longer stimulated and hence will miss details and fail to find creative solutions or make necessary changes. In order to keep the brain creative and optimally functioning Hüther recommends regular changes within an organisation or within each department.[1] This will ensure better brains in the business.

---

[1] See our discussion of job rotation in Chap. 5.3.2.

2. **Network corporate knowledge**

   Creative solutions can normally be found within the current knowledge of organisations. Indeed organisations have immense amounts of brainpower and knowledge sitting in the individuals in the organisation and this is normally underused. Hüther recommends creating teams that are cross-departmental and stresses the value of large conferences that give new impulses, show different perspectives and the following exchange and discussion can activate neuronal networks that would otherwise remain passive. It is important for employees to be able to profit from the knowledge of each other and this must be tied into organisational planning.

3. **Develop a positive mistake culture**

   If employees are punished for their mistakes this can create fear and insecurity in the workplace. As we mentioned (see Sect. 2.7.2) fear stimulates one of the three instinctive fear reactions: fight, flight, or freeze. Aside from this we also know that fear causes other distortions in the brain. This is why employees need to be given the opportunity to learn from their mistakes. Fear of sanctions can cause more distortion in the system and management needs to ensure that employees do not feel this pressure and fear of failure.

4. **Create space for positive experiences**

   Management and leaders should build and develop strong relationships with employees through praise, thanks and supportive behaviours. This activates networks of positive experiences and their emotions—stimulating whole positive circuits in the brain. This will also stimulate connections to other networks and allow access to more information but also increase motivation.

   The supportive leader shows three qualities:

   - They encourage employees to take on new tasks and challenges. This is to motivate employees at a more emotional level, this is especially important for employees who lack courage or motivation. This may mean changing the basic attitudes of some of these employees and these "unproductive" employees need to be treated with respect.
   - They encourage employees to tackle tasks and problems and trust them to find and create their own good solutions. This means that management must also have enough courage to trust their own employees.
   - They inspire their employees and help them to develop motivation for their functions and tasks. This also means that the management and leaders are able to keep their own motivation high but also to be able to keep passing this on to their employees.

   A leader who lives these principles sees employees less as resources but more as a potential to be developed. This form of leadership requires, by necessity, tolerance, courage and trust in yourself and in others. Behaviours that compensate for weaknesses such as sanctions, pressure and hierarchical command structures should, according to Hüther, become obsolete.

3.4   David Rock's SCARF Model

David Rock's SCARF model (Rock 2008) builds on the understanding that the brain is focused on increasing or sustaining reward and avoiding negative experiences. From this focus on reward and avoidance of negativity develop various drives and behaviours in the workplace. This is split into five categories:

1. **Status**

   By status David Rock does not just mean the hierarchical status but rather how in interpersonal relationships and individuals reward centre will be activated. When employees are given praise or criticism this will influence their status. The feeling of threat is individually processed very differently between different people—a small "tip" given, for some, for example, can already be seen as a threat and stimulate a defensive reaction.

   That status is only possible through hierarchical promotion in organisations is a general misconception. David Rock states that, alternatively, positive feedback is a much more positive way to generate wider status effects. This stimulates the brain, its reward centres and creates a positive environment for the brain.

2. **Certainty**

   The brain is continually scanning the environment to make predictions about the future and to predict outcomes from the patterns it recognises. In familiar situations the brain uses less resources than in unfamiliar situations. This means that in unfamiliar situations the brain will be strained, it will be uncomfortable.

   In familiar situations where the outcomes are predictable the reward system will be activated and a feeling of security will be generated. This is why Rock recommends clear communication in periods of change and breaking down of large processes into smaller processes that can be clearly seen and understood. An important part of this is the setting of clear goals and milestones.

3. **Autonomy**

   With autonomy employees have the ability to freely influence and design their workplace. Lack of autonomy can be processed as a threat situation and hence will promote stress and its negative implications in the brain. Employees should be given as much autonomy as it is possible to give. This can involve various elements such as managers interfering as little as possible and giving as much free room as possible including, as much as feasible, the free choice of working hours and design in the workplace. Interestingly just being promised more autonomy will activate the reward system in the brain.

4. **Relatedness**

   The social wiring in our brains means that we in daily life, and in business, form social groups and build relationships. These groups build mutual trust and form a barrier against the unknown. These feelings and the interpersonal bonding promote the production of oxytocin, the trust and bonding hormone, which increases the positive feeling of trust and stabilizes these relationships. Therefore trust and bonding should be actively promoted in business by ensuring that employees can work in small project teams and allow the building of relationships. Coaching programmes can also be positive stimulus to this trust and bonding system.

5. **Fairness**

Unfairness stimulates a strong emotional reaction in the brain, an automatic defence mechanism. This emotional reaction can for example, be shut down, with punishment of the source of the unfairness. This activates the reward centre in the brain and counteracts the negative impact of unfairness. This feeling of unfairness can unintentionally be promoted in corporations through unclear and intransparent communication. It is also a key function of senior management to form joint rules of conduct and to ensure that no department or part of the organisation is treated differently.

3.5   Neuroleadership According to Elger

Elger in his book "Neuroleadership" (Elger 2009) goes into the brain and numerous scientific studies and defines four basic systems in the brain: the reward system, the emotional system, the memory system and the decision system. Basing his work on scientific studies Elger shows how these work together and how they can be applied to daily business. From this he has developed seven base principles of neuroleadership:

1. **The reward system**

Activating the reward system of employees is of central importance. The reward system generates feelings of comfort, happiness and satisfaction and even if it is permanently stimulated does not lead to habituation. Factors that influence this are, for example, working atmosphere, harmonious relationships with co-workers and management, type and form of tasks and the design of the workplace.

2. **Fairness und feedback**

The brain, as a social organ, strives for fairness and will actively try to keep this balance. If the brain, and the person, feels unfairness then the person will actively try to balance this out and seek justice (altruistic punishment). Positive feedback will activate the brain's reward system and minimise the need for altruistic punishment and a more positive working environment.

3. **Influence through information**

The brain is continually making evaluations from any situation it encounters and from this also makes prediction. This means the brain is constantly looking for information that can help it to make predictions that can be processed positively or negatively. This means that in corporations the impact of important decisions needs to be well thought through and how this is communicated is relevant to the impact while transparency needs to be guaranteed at all times.

4. **Each brain is unique**

Each and every brain has its own structure that is formed from a series of interconnected networks that have been laid down from personal experiences that are different from person to person. These give rise to an endless multitude of perspectives and ways of processing individual information. It is therefore essential that leaders understand how their employees operate and think. This requires good people skills, understanding of how humans operate and plenty of common sense and a good gut feeling.

5. **Facts are tied to emotions**
   All information is processed and related unconsciously to various emotional stimuli. Emotions are the base of human beings and therefore information is only processed in relation to these emotions. This information is then compared and balanced and saved according to various emotions—this is an unconscious process. Retrieving this information is therefore to varying degrees an emotional experience and will generate various behaviours according to these emotions. This means that leaders need to focus on the emotional aspects of leadership to be able to positively influence their employees.

6. **Experience defines our behaviour**
   Experiences give rise to varying emotions and behaviours and thus if we can draw on positive experiences and ways of behaving then we will be able to deal with our tasks better and more efficiently. This will also create a better environment and better control of stress. This will also ensure that positive experiences are a part of the workplace will enable employees to lay down networks tying into the positive experiences and the respective behaviours.

7. **Situational dynamics**
   The brain prefers situational behaviours based on emotional stimuli rather than planned behaviours. This means that in given situations people will behave differently according to the emotional dynamics. This means in leadership situational dynamics should be dealt with intuitively and allowed to develop and spontaneously bubble up but uncontrolled dynamics need to be avoided through good planning and strong emotional understanding of the emotional power and potential dynamics of certain situations.

3.6 Pillay's Brain Based Approach

Srinivasan Pillay is a recent addition to the neuroleadership market and a reflection of the number of people of higher qualifications that are entering into the market. Pillay studied at Harvard Medical School and has a background in neuroscience and clinical psychiatry—Pillay, for example, was head of the panic disorders research programme in brain imaging. Though focusing primarily on the coaching market and personal development, his approach has taken a much more detailed and fundamental approach than that of other protagonists in the field. He peers into the brain at much more detail and gives brain-based explanation for various situations and their solutions. His book "Life Unlocked" (Pillay 2010) is a book on personal mastery and mastering fear and is also very relevant for business coaches. But of direct relevance to neuroleadership his book "Your Brain and Business"

(Pillay 2011) which takes readers into the details of the brain in business and into the following areas:
– Positive and negative thinking
– Social intelligence and effective relationships
– Innovation and intuition
– Form ideas to action orientation
– Form action orientation to change
– Coaching brain regions
– Coaching brain processes

Pillay takes readers into much more depth of the brain than other figures in the field and ties his approaches to a wealth of scientific knowledge. For example in the introduction to change he notes the competing forces in the brain and concepts such as biased choice value and how conditioning take place. He notes that the brain will need to get to action orientation and that various brain processes can block this be it short term memory located in the dorsolateral prefrontal cortex, emotional contexts and activating the premotor cortex.

Pillay has also developed various approaches for dealing with specific brain regions. For example he has interventions designed to deal with the amygdala, short term-memory, basal ganglia and reward systems, corpus callosum (the brain bridge connecting the two hemispheres) and more.

His approach can be summarised as:
– Identify mental state (e.g. fear)
– Describe this in terms of brain regions and activation
– Intervention based on research into brain regions in previous stage

His approach is therefore a detailed brain-focused approach drawing on a neuroscientific research and his personal experience as a clinical psychiatrist. Despite the detail, his approaches are practical and informative to coaches, leadership development experts and managers alike. However, as his approach is specific, it may lack the general applicability of other approaches.

3.7   Evaluation of the Approaches

There has been an explosion of books in recent years focusing on various aspects of the brain and the impact on human beings, decision-making, health, buying, influence, to name but a few applications. Some of these have been targeted at the general market and have become international best sellers. These include "Blink" by Malcolm Gladwell looking at our intuitive decision making, "How we Decide" and "Proust was a Neuroscientist" by Jonah Lehrer that look more specifically into the brain and he relates these to decision-making processes and sensory processes respectively. These have been huge hits and quite rightly so. They are well researched, very readable and informative. Martin Lindstrom has targeted a more general audience with his books into neuromarketing: "Buyology" also being a major international best seller—a fascinating read into the brain and how consumers make decisions and can be influenced by targeted approaches into the brain. Yet these types of books, though having a general application to business administration, do not go into the specifics of business management. There is also a large field looking into the brain and mindfulness, the calm mind and general health. Some are well researched and well written others not. Yet, though these lend momentum to the "neuro" scene and are informative and fascinating, they do not approach specifics of business administration. This is why we have not looked into these, interesting as many are, and have singled out the specific approaches outlined previously.

These approaches have more specific applications for the business administration field and for leadership. There are many similarities between them, as there must be if the brain is the basis. We feel that though neuroleadership is not a term fixed in the business realm there is growing body of research and applications which make these very relevant and the research is easily applicable to the business context and that this can fundamentally change our perspective of doing business.

Hermann with his approach singled out the brain as the basis for differences in ways of treating information and this has provided a strong basis for measurements of the types of people operating in teams and in organisations. This in some ways, arguably, may contradict the complex man theory and brain-directed man views of man. After all the classification of people into four simple categories is not a complex man theory and many have criticized this as being too simple. Indeed this is a valid criticism. Yet at the same time the value of his model is that he was one of the first to really look at the brain and not the psychological manifestations and apply this to a simplified model which helps us to understand personal differences. This is one of the most important, and underestimated values, of such psychometric testing tools, the simple understanding that we are different and this is neither correct nor incorrect and can have its strengths and weaknesses, this understanding in itself will create more harmonious working places.

As we mentioned in Sect. 3.2 his model has been criticised by neuroscientists for its over simplicity and for its lack of verification of validity and its claims and yet we know that brain lateralisation is one of the distinguishing feature of the brain. As simple as this may seem, it holds very true and there is a vast body of research that points to this lateralisation. The left amygdala, for example, will process specifics of fear (e.g. fearful eyes) and the right amygdale the general environment of fear (Hardee et al. 2008). This suggests that in the complexity of the brain some things are simpler than we like to make out. His approach though does only classify four types which we know intuitively will be wrong and what many of the other figures in the field are saying is that we must remember that each mind is individual (he does, however, also say this himself). His approach also does not go into the specifics of leading but rather into the creative and team forming aspects of businesses. This in itself is useful but will not help style a brain friendly environment or brain friendly approaches to leadership.

Hüther, through his background in neurology, brings fundamental understanding of the brain and has placed this into business contexts. This is a valuable approach and is backed up by solid scientific findings. His view has taken a general approach to the environment of business and generalities of human behaviour and how we as leaders can influence the environment and importantly why and what the consequences are if we do and if we do not operate in this fashion.

Elger has also taken a look into business and himself introduced the term neuroleadership to the German-speaking world with his book "Neuroleadership". He also has a solid background but, interestingly, in dealing with epilepsy. His approach goes into some more details and looks more at the individual's brain than broader environmental aspects as Hüther does. He takes an approach of looking into the individual's brains and provides a simple framework for understanding the base function of brains and applying this in a more general way in business.

Similarly David Rock has also taken a model and approach that looks at the behaviours of people in the system and how the leaders can approach this. David Rock's background into coaching focused on the behavioural aspects of this and how we can implement a brain friendly and brain suitable environment that will enable people's brains to function optimally and avoid many of the problems that plague many businesses such as lack of trust or underlying resentment. His coaching approach also focuses on changing the approaches of individual leaders and also of focusing on one's own brain. In many of these aspects it is easy to forget that it is not just the brains of the employees we should be looking into but also the brains of the leaders themselves as these will be open to the same influences. This approach to coaching and his SCARF model is a shift in paradigm for many leaders and an important shift for if we want the business to have good brains doing good things, these brains must be functioning optimally at whatever level.

Srinivasan Pillay's approach is much more specific. He moves away from generalities that may be hard and a little elusive to implement as they lack concrete details (not that this approach is invalid—it is very valid). Through this we can gain specific brain-based insights into the very neural substrates of, for example, making a commitment to a decision and from this identify methods and approaches to influence this. Understanding the neural basis of these can give clear insights into the specifics of human behaviour with very specific interventions. This is solidly and scientifically backed up and in this scientific approach there are fewer generalities and more specifics. From this Pillay has developed different approaches to deal with specific situations such as creativity, fear, sales and, for example, mergers and acquisitions. This is an approach which may be more accessible to the specifics of business and many leaders who want specific interventions may be more attracted to this approach.

Pillay has also developed some very focused coaching protocols for specific brain interventions e.g. a fear intervention based on amygdala over activation will approach fear through using the knowledge of how fear is processed in the brain (see Sect. 2.7.2) and especially designed to counteract this Table 3.1.

These approaches though seemingly different are all based on the same object: the human brain. Their approaches show many parallels looking at Hüther, Elger, Rock and Pillay we can see some large overlapping areas which are formulated and approached in different ways. All know that fear is bad and can cause various distortions and negative reactions in the brain and in our behaviours. Reward is the base for learning as are positive brain environments, unfairness is to be avoided and causes its own form of distortion in the brain and trust needs to be built and is the

Table 3.1 Summary of the approaches

	Herrmann	Hüther	Elger	Rock	Pillay
Description	Brain dominance concept	Supportive leadership	Neuroleadership	SCARF model	Brain focused interventions
Basis	Hemisphere lateralisation and limbic system	Selected neurobiological processes	Four basic brain systems	Activation of the reward system	Specific neural substrates of relevant situations
Approach for organisational and personnel development	Consideration of dominating brain region: Rational Safety-focused Feeling Experimental	Challenge Network knowledge Positive mistake culture Positive experiences	Reward system Fairness and feedback Information Individuality Emotions Experiences Dynamics of situations	Status Certainty Autonomy Relatedness Fairness	Specific situations Underlying brain processes of these situations Neural substrates of these brain processes Interventions based on scientific knowledge of these substrates

basis for all solid business interactions. The similarities are astounding as indeed they should be if they are indeed dealing with the brain and if they all do have a clear understanding of how the brain works. Their findings have been formulated differently focusing on different aspects. Some approach more broader aspects (Hüther) and some approach more specific aspects (Pillay). They however provide the groundwork for the basis of neuroleadership using the insights from brain science in business administration, in management and in leadership.

The Current Trend in Leadership: Neurocoaching
In recent years the term neurocoaching has been taken up rapidly by the coaching community. The speed of this has been complemented by a variety of techniques and methods also popping up. These methods and approaches all focus on the brain and the research into cognitive ability and emotional processes in the brain to improve the brain of the coachee. This is a classification of the approaches:

Technically Supported Methods
These methods use various techniques such as audio recordings but more recently so-called mind machines. These are designed to improve the functioning of the brain and stimulate a better communication specifically between the hemispheres. Some also claim to be able to stimulate the alpha state or deeper states of relaxation which is popularly ascribed to powerful moments of inspiration and intuition. Though the claims are often exaggerated by some that are aggressively marketed, evidence does support their effect on relaxation and anxiety particularly. Neurofeedback is also reaching a broader and more scientific field—these techniques use simplified EEG tools to train the brain's ability to tap into various mental states. Some of these techniques have had considerable success in treating milder forms of autism (Asperger's Syndrome), for example (Thompson et al. 2010).

"Train Your Brain" Programmes
These types of coaching and training programmes target cognitive abilities through various training exercises mostly done on a computer. These range from the popular brain jogging type of exercises on popular games consoles such as Nintendo to more serious scientific tools. Though thrown into the spotlight with powerful claims by the producers and a hungry public, particularly the aging population keen to reduce the effects of aging, most research shows limited effects of these (Owen et al. 2010; Mann 2010). *Though the classic neuroscientists adage of "What fires together wires together" seems to support continual cognitive practice and the old proverb "use it or lose it" holds true to some extent. More serious programmes target, for example, fluid intelligence which is scientifically better researched and is shown to improve IQ* (Sternberg 2008) *and is transferable to other tasks.*

Neuroassociative Training
This approach taps into the brain's ability to build associations. This can be approached in two dimensions: 1. The associations that we have built up and that may need to be "reprogrammed" 2. The ability to build new associations to improve and unleash potential new behaviours. This is often linked to neurolinguistic programming (NLP). This was much popularised particularly in the 1990's but does not a have a solid reputation in the scientific community many claiming it is pseudo-science and should be discredited. Yet, that

said, some recent neuroscientific study coming out does support what NLP has proposed.[2] Another specific model, though less widespread, is the Zurich Resource Model which is a specifically designed coaching methodology developed by psychotherapists at Zurich University that takes into account the brain's ability to build associations (Storch 2004).

Integrative Stress Management
In combination with recent research into stress new methodologies are being formed that focus on enabling employees to better deal with stress and to become more resilient. These are based on solid scientific research into the brain and are used to coach employees to better be able to control their cognitive and emotional processes in the brain.

Brain-Targeted Interventions
With the likes of Srinivasan Pillay there are some protagonists in the field now focusing on more specific interventions supported by brain science. These will involve a specific focus on brain regions and their specific manifestations. For example, fear and anxiety will involve an amygdala intervention coaching programme. Lack of trust will involve a reward centre and oxytocin promoting intervention and inability to make decisions will involve a ventromedial prefrontal cortex intervention that targets the ability to balance incoming information and come to a decision.

In this rapidly growing sea of information and popular science it is important to understand what the specific relevance will be for neuroleadership and specifically what impact this will have on leading people in organisations. There needs particularly to be an approach that takes this, away from popular science (as interesting as this may be), into a concrete business administration context and shows how a brain based approach will provide clearer and/or more value than standard approaches to organisational and personnel management.

To bridge this gap we will now go into systematically using the knowledge of the brain to develop an approach that supports brain science and organisational development by using the four basic human needs. We will draw on the work of Klaus

---

[2] "Neuro-Linguistic Programming: A Critical Appreciation for Managers and Developers" by Paul Tosey and Jane Mathison is an introduction and serious discussion of its tools and their scientific grounding.

Grawe whose work into neuropsychotherapy takes the latest research into brain science and ties this to psychotherapeutic work. His work into these basic needs is therefore strongly founded on neuroscience and psychology and therapy alike. Satisfying these basic needs will lead to an activation of the reward system in the brain and so build an environment that is brain friendly and thus allow the brain to operate at a better level and to generate the positive feeling within an organisation that will support its effective and efficient functioning. This will help develop the individual and management but also lead to better business results because with optimally balanced brains, collaboration, trust, creativity and motivation will be optimally tapped into. This can only be better for businesses of all sizes.

3.8   Summary

- Neuroscientific approaches in corporate contexts have been approached, amongst others, by:
    - Herrmann and his **Brain Dominance Instrument**—a self-reporting test that shows your thinking and cognitive preferences according to a brain based model.
    - **Hüther** with **supportive leadership** has developed concepts that, based on neuroscience, make recommendations on how to support employees in their development and how they can develop their potential.
    - **David Rock's SCARF Model** formulates five dimensions that need to be considered (Status, Certainty, Autonomy, Relatedness, Fairness). This is based on neuroscientific studies and practical experience in the business field.
    - **Elger** summarises insights into neuroscience and business applications into **seven base rules for leaders**. These include: reward system, fairness and feedback, information, individuality of brains, experiences drive behaviours. These all influence the dynamics of various situations in business.
    - **Srinivasan Pillay's** approach is based on specific knowledge of neural substrates and is thus a **targeted regional approach** to brain science in business scenarios. He also focuses heavily on specific interventions for leaders and for coaches.
- The number of approaches show parallels and from this we can define recommendations for implementations in business contexts.
- Neurocoaching is a recent trend using the research into the brain to apply to coaching and developmental contexts.
    - Technically supported methods
    - Brain training programmes
    - Neuroassociative training and coaching
    - Integrative stress management
    - Brain-targeted interventions

Four Basic Human Needs at the Heart of Neuroscience

4

The brain is a complex organ and the variations in human behaviour are also a seemingly endless sea of subtle differences. This poses many challenges in trying to find clearer answers to human behaviour in any context but also specifically in the context of business administration. This chapter therefore aims to go to the basis of human behaviour. We draw on the work of Klaus Grawe to highlight how neuroscience has combined with psychotherapy and psychology to understand what the very neural substrates are at the basis of human behaviour. This chapter takes us through what we can see as the neuroscientifically founded basic needs of human beings and how this will subsequently influence each of our motivational behaviours and hence our way of interacting with the world around us.

Objectives

- Understand the relevance of basic needs
- Describe the four basic needs and their background and impact on human behaviour
- Understand how these affect our motivational behaviours
- Understand how these are formed into the consistency theory model

4.1 Introduction

It is the role of the neuroleader to understand these individual processes from the view of the brain and an individual's brain: it is also the role of the leader to understand their employees. We know the brain is an emotionally driven organ and so a neuroleader can only hope to be able to tap into the full power of the brain of their employees through understanding their dreams, visions and what drives each employee emotionally.

In Chap. 2 we looked into the brain and learned about some of its basic organisation and ways of communication. We noted some specific functional aspects such as the reward system but also the HTPA stress axis and how fear

A. Ghadiri et al., *Neuroleadership*, Management for Professionals,
DOI 10.1007/978-3-642-30165-0_4, © Springer-Verlag Berlin Heidelberg 2012

impacts the brain. We also noted that the environment and experiences a person has will develop a person's given brain—this ties into the knowledge of how the brain is forever plastic and that our neurons are organically connecting, reconnecting and growing at any given time. This growth is dependant on the stimuli that the brain is processing at any given time. We noted that there is a constant interaction between the brain and the environment and both will influence each other (Sect. 2.10).

Given this, the question we need to ask is: how can we know how the brain will react in a given context and how can we know about the "action" of brains in general? Is this realistic? It is realistic because the research shows a number of important facts: the brain develops in similar ways—all healthy human beings have the same brain structures that are responsible for the same processes. The connections are predefined—the ways these are used are what will differ between individuals and the intensity that they are used will define how they grow relative to each other.

However, to gain a deeper fundamental understanding of the brain and its base functioning we will look into psychology. Indeed there needs to be a close link to psychology. Psychology after all looks into the forms and laws of personal experience and behaviour. These various forms of perceptions, experience and behaviour are manifested in an endless multitude of ways between individuals. This is simply because the environment and its stimuli are perceived and processed differently by each individual (Feist & Primis 2010). Neuroscience complements psychology and looks deeper and from a different angle into these perceptions and behaviours and cognitive psychologists and cognitive neuroscientists look into the very neural substrates of such behaviours (Gazzaniga et al. 2008). We can now see that many behaviours are not processed differently but that the processing that drives certain reactions and behaviours is similar. Neural correlates therefore drive psychology. The reaction to a stimulus however remains different. Fear, for example, is processed as fear (as outlined in Sect. 2.7.2) but in many situations individuals will not see fear but may, for example, see a challenge. If, as we are seeing, psychological processes lie on neural processes then understanding this offers a variety of ways to influence the environment in corporations in which employees operate.[1]

Since the times of Freud there has been an ever-increasing body of research into the brain and psychology and therapy. Many theories over the last century have focused on single drivers—much like the concepts of man mentioned in Chap. 1. Yet what the research has shown is that there are a number of drives that drive us at a primitive (natural) level but specifically at an emotional psychological level. We do stress that we are not implying that neuroleadership be a psychological or therapeutic process but that the insights in these fields can also give us a powerful understanding of human nature in the context of the brain and enhance our ability to

---

[1] For the sake of simplicity we have not differentiated here between psychology and organisational psychology whereby organisational psychology looks into the experience and perceptions of individuals in organisations.

tap into this in business contexts. The work of the German psychotherapy researcher Klaus Grawe has reached, we see, the culmination of this knowledge. Klaus Grawe is one of the founders of neuropsychotherapy and his focus on neuropsychotherapy means that he could draw on the knowledge of psychology and psychotherapy but also on the biological basis of the brain (Freud incidentally was also an excellent neurologist). He has therefore combined the current state of knowledge on the brain and that of psychology and formed this into a unified theory of the basic needs of human beings and the following motivational schemata (Grawe 2006). This draws strongly on Seymour Epstein's Cognitive-Experiential Self-Theory (Epstein and Weiner 2003) that outlines four basic needs—combining basic needs that psychologists and therapists have separately defined as being at the core of human nature. Epstein noted in what is, in retrospect, a simple insight that we do not have a single need but multiple needs and that Freud (the pleasure principle, see Sect. 4.2.4) was as correct as Bowlby (see Sect. 4.2.1) was with his attachment theory.

This model of basic needs is of particular relevance to us in neuroleadership. Indeed we see it as crucial. We see it as crucial because in leadership contexts we are dealing with human beings and their ability to be motivated, to perform and to engage in the work assigned to them. If we can understand the very neural substrates of the human mind and moreover the basis of human interactions then we can understand where we can apply the point of leverage. Grawe's model of basic needs and his subsequent consistency theory model is solidly founded in neuroscientific research and gives us a clear model at the very core of human behaviour. In learning to tap into these basic needs we have the core of neuroleadership—tapping into the core of human beings and understanding their representations on motivational drives and goals. We take this and place this onto organisational and personnel development models in Chap. 5. This will also highlight how and why different people will react differently to the different tools.

We will therefore now look into these basic needs of human beings. The needs that drive our satisfaction, well-being, and fulfilment—this core of human behaviour. To fulfil these basic needs, each individual will develop their own approach—to search for positive experiences and avoid negative experiences. These are known as motivational schemata and we will discuss these in more detail in the following sections before going into Grawe's consistency model itself.

4.2   Basic Needs

From an evolutionary perspective human functions have developed so as to use the environment to its best and allow the reproduction and development of the species—its survival and growth. This raises the question of what is precisely the optimal condition for human development. These are in a first step the physiological basic needs that drive our physical survival: hunger, thirst and sleep. This is the base of the pyramid in Maslow's model we mentioned in Sect. 1.5.3. These needs have been extensively researched in many forms. On the other side our psychological

Fig. 4.1 Reciprocal influence of the basic needs

needs are represented by many different approaches and interpretations. Grawe and Epstein defined four basic needs, as we have just outlined, and Grawe defined these as, "Needs that are present among all humans, and their violation or enduring nonfulfillment leads to impairments in mental health and well-being." (Grawe 2006). These are:

- The need for attachment
- The need for orientation and control
- The need for self-esteem and its protection and development
- The need for pleasure and avoidance of pain

These four needs are closely related to each other and the satisfaction of one will influence the others (See Fig. 4.1).

It is necessary to look at the basic needs individually as each need stimulates different neuronal circuits and will activate different regions of the brain. We will follow this with a discussion of the four basic needs.

4.2.1   Attachment

The attachment and bonding need of humans is the best-researched need in neuroscience. This need for attachment and an attachment person to bond with takes effect from birth onwards and these will be laid down in our brain and our memory. This means that our perceptions, behaviours and emotional reactions and motivations can be laid down very early in life. This is directly linked to the availability of an attachment figure, which is usually one of the primary caregivers, for normal social and emotional development. If this is not the case this will have a negative influence on the fulfilment of this need for attachment.

Much early work on this was done by John Bowlby starting in the 1950s (with a report of the World Health Organisation on "Maternal Care and Mental Health" (Bowlby 1951)) and later supported by work from Mary Ainsworth (Bowlby et al. 1992). The current attachment theory defines four models of attachment which can be ascribed to behaviours in adults. The attachment patterns are: secure, avoidant, ambivalent and disorganised. Bowlby was, surprisingly now, ostracised by the psychoanalytic community for his work as it went against the current theories of the time. It has now become broadly accepted and has a mass of empirical research behind it.

> *A large corporation introduces a new employee on their first day to a mentor that will accompany them. The mentor has been with the company for a long time and knows the structure, the rituals, processes, symbols and idiosyncrasies of the company. On a personal level the mentor will introduce the new employee to the company and its characteristics. The mentor is also available for problems of a corporate and a personal level. The mentor is also a trusting figure that this new employee can turn to in times of uncertainty, as the mentor is not a part of the hierarchical command structure. This is therefore a proactive approach of the company to introduce an initial bonding figure that can support a new employee.*

Neurobiological research shows clearly the high importance of bonding particularly in early years. In research into animal behaviour, animals show stress reactions in new and unfamiliar environments. Research, around the time of Bowlby's work on attachment theory (by Harry Harlow), with monkeys showed that baby monkeys brought up in solitary confinement developed distorted behaviours. When these babies had a steel model of an adult monkey placed in their cage covered in fur the baby chimp immediately went to this and spent a lot of their time cuddled up with it. Even this model "mother" helped improve their behaviour and condition (Harlow 1958).

The hormone that has been discovered to influence this strongly is the so-called bonding hormone oxytocin. Oxytocin is released in huge amounts in women during labour and is passed on to the freshly born baby in large doses in their first suckling of breast milk (Matthiesen et al. 2001). This is the first initial boost to bonding for both mother and child immediately after childbirth. Oxytocin has also been researched in mating behaviours and is considered (especially) in pop psychology as a "bonding hormone" or "love hormone" depending on whose version you read. Though these claims may be exaggerated it is implicated strongly in both bonding and sexual desire (Carmichael et al. 1987; Palmer 2002).

Trust similarly stimulates oxytocin and hence it is also seen as the trust hormone. Trust we can see as a bonding element also and hence the importance of building trust in organisations. A study by Kosfeld, Heinrichs, Zak, Fischbacher und Fehr in 2005 (Kosfeld et al. 2005) showed an increase in trusting behaviour after individuals had received oxytocin in the form of a nasal spray. This was further supported by a study in 2010 (Kosfeld et al. 2005) that showed an increase in trusting behaviours in groups. Oxytocin increases the group cohesion and harmony and can be expressed in the form of trust, love and calmness. Against non-group members a defensive rather than an offensive aggressive behaviour is expressed.

> *Especially at the start of a new job when insecurities are the highest the importance of an attachment person is at the highest also. The reference person need not necessarily be the manager or leader themselves, it can be a team member, a formal mentor or a contact person in Human Resources. In some larger corporations there are specific mentoring programmes but this need not be so formally organised and can simple be a so-called "uncle" in a project team.*

4.2.2   Orientation and Control

Everyone has a need for orientation and control. This translates as the ability for an individual to design and develop their own environment. We can, in a different context, think of our need or desire to build our own a house or simply furnish our own house and create our own way of functioning as a family. Imagine having to have a state controlled design system for our flats, houses or even gardens. This is our own desire to live and control our own environment. This is our basic urge to be able to control our environment to develop our personal area of impact and to be able to avoid external control. Yet some form of external control and particularly orientation is important also. This allows a person to be able to know where they are and where they are going—to know where we tie into the bigger scheme of things. This is particularly important in organisations and when we need to achieve certain goals. We need to know where we are and where we are going—this also helps us to feel in control and to be able to proactively move forward. We can see it as an existential need for the control of our environment and indeed our future and this is why employees have the drive and fundamental need to know about what is happening, about the changes and direction a corporation is taking.

Thanks, also to the mentor the new employee has been able to start and integrate well into the new corporation. This individual has already formed various friendly relationships with colleagues and is already leading their first project. This individual has also been given enough free room and autonomy to solve their tasks. They are in the position to make operative decisions and to lead the project independently. The leader has ensured that the goals of the project are aligned with the corporation and the needs of the business. This employee is clearly informed of what needs to be achieved and has access to the information that is necessary and all decisions that influence them and their project.

If a situation is unclear and ambiguous this will stimulate a negative reaction in the limbic system, specifically the amygdala (Whalen 1998) This will stimulate an immediate fear reaction as we detailed in Sect. 2.7.2.1. If this stress reaction can be controlled and mastered this may stimulate reward circuits and be saved as a learning memory. However, if this cannot be controlled this can destabilise the neuronal circuits and trigger a negative cycle of thought processes and potentially also of a conditioning circuit—that means development of a negative trigger stimulated with an unrelated stimuli. This can lead to a conditioning and fear of unknown situations which in turn will increase the negative stimuli and further decrease the ability to deal with this (see Sect. 2.5.1).

Transparency, clarity and the specific goals of tasks are necessary for employees to be able to effectively and efficiently deal with their specific tasks and this is the role of leadership to communicate this well. The basic need for orientation will be damaged as soon as the goals are unclear and information is ambiguous. The resulting insecurity can then stimulate a stress reaction, as has previously been outlined, and this will likely have a negative impact on the job and its completion. It is also important that employees have enough flexibility and room for manoeuvre so that they can exert as much control as possible over the task. Micro management and continual checking will exert a negative influence on this.

4.2.3   Self-Esteem

The need for self-esteem differs from the other needs in that it is a specific human need. Individuals are constantly looking to increase their self worth and protect this also. This is only possible through having the ability to reflect and be able to perceive this and so to cognizize this. Through our interactions with others our own self image is formed and our self worth is part of this self image that is influenced by this complex net of interactions with others in the environment and their reactions and observations with each of us. We therefore develop a perception but also a need for value (Cast and Burke 2002). Therefore, because of its complexity and difficulty to research this at a neuroscientific level (with moral and ethical constraints) there has been relatively little neuroscientific research into self-esteem and self-worth (Grawe 2006). Nevertheless this has expanded more recently (Somerville et al. 2010; Eisenberger et al. 2011; Korsten et al. 2007). Recent work has also analysed some of the neural correlates particularly in contexts of social acceptance and rejection (Gyurak et al. 2011).

The first project for this new employee went successfully. They made the correct decisions and their assumptions and predictions were also accurate. Their superior praised their ability and the success of the project. Colleagues and collaborators shared the praise as this was also communicated at the departmental level. This new employee was especially satisfied as they had always been an ambitious and dedicated worker and had always striven to make the best out of their work and is generally only satisfied with the successful completion of a project.

Some people, with low self-esteem, may seem to avoid all actions that could lead to higher self-esteem. This can be the result of previous painful experiences that have led to a defensive reactions and an inhibition to take on new tasks and challenges that could potentially lead to another feeling of insufficiency and hence lower even further self-esteem. This can be positioned as a strategy to at least preserve self-esteem by avoiding risky behaviour that could damage it even further. This in itself illustrates the complexity and individuality of such experiences which can be based on a whole scheme of previous experiences. It is also possible that a deficiency in one basic need may be balanced out in the other basic needs so that the effort in one may be so compensated (Grawe 2006). An observable phenomenon is that of employees with little self-esteem compensating this through increased control and precise ideas of how regulations and rules should be implemented.

With employees that are ambitious, as this new employee, they will continually strive to improve their self-esteem through their work and the successful completion of a project will be particularly motivating. Other factors will also play a role—the recognition and appreciation at a higher level specifically. The comparison and interaction with other employees will additionally increase their personal motivation and encourage them to actively achieve their goals.

4.2.4   Pleasure and Pain Avoidance

With the basic need of pleasure maximisation and pain avoidance human beings follow the simple logic that we aim to increase pleasure and avoid unpleasurable, dangerous or painful experiences. Our experience over time have given rise to a whole network of mostly unconscious triggers and associations that are linked to either positive or negative experiences and pleasure and pain respectively. These subjective experiences will colour our view of the world. This is clearly a subjective and not an objective area.

> *This new employee has experienced that teamwork in the new corporation functions particularly well. The senior leadership make sure that the teams are well designed and that the composition is harmonious. The new employee has already been involved with two particularly successful projects with cooperative and competent project members from various departments. The leadership team has been actively involved in generating the positive atmosphere with joint meals and events that have encouraged interaction in social contexts and have actively connected with the individuals. This individual has therefore had the experience of being involved in successful projects and bringing these to successful completion (objective criteria) but also that the teams have harmonised well together and that the work is particularly enjoyable (subjective criteria).*

This internal rating process ties in to neuronal processes. New stimuli in the brain will be compared to previous stimuli and this will stimulate various neuronal circuits based on our previous experiences. The limbic system operates in coordination with other brain regions as a rating central for stimuli and their satisfaction or non-completion and this fulfilment or failure to fulfil this basic need will influence the behaviour of individuals (see Sect. 2.4). This clearly ties into the processes we spoke about of reward in Sect. 2.5.2 and the respective important learning impact but also of anxiety and stress which are the opposite of this. This is one of Freud's base theories (the pleasure principle).

> *The managing team is careful to put teams together not only based on the competencies and skills of the future team members but also with relevance to their personal skills and experience to ensure that the teams work well together. The management focuses on the tasks and on the relationships to help develop positive working standards and ethics. These positive experiences made by team members lead to positive memories and positive schemes laid down which means that this will influence future collaborations positively.*

4.3   Summarising the Basic Needs

As we noted these four basic needs lie at the emotional heart of human beings. They differ slightly but are also related to the survival instincts which lie at a primitive and deeper level in the brain. We can think of the survival instincts as the brain stem and the emotional needs as the next level, the limbic level—if we were relating these to the three-layer model of the brain we outlined in Sect. 2.1. As we mentioned here the brain is interlinked and so survival needs will colour our emotional needs and emotional needs may colour each other—these may also

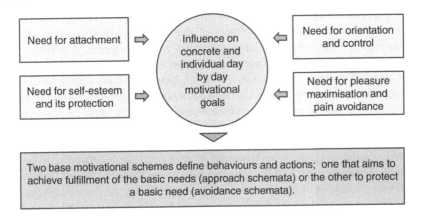

Fig. 4.2 Factors influencing human behaviour

work in separation. The reward centre which is directly linked to pleasure, as we noted in Sect. 2.5.2, is also stimulated by primary rewards, our survival instincts, food and sex for example. Fulfilment of one or more basic needs will also stimulate reward and hence colour the basic need for pleasure. For example being complimented will also influence our basic need for self-esteem, but it will also be a rewarding experience, increasing our pleasure. The same applies to attachment and orientation and control—these can all stimulate reward and hence pleasure. If these needs are not fulfilled or in balance then a person cannot be in harmony and this will manifest itself in disruptive behaviour and well being (and in more extreme cases to psychological disorders).

We will now look into motivational schemata: the basic needs describe our interaction with the world around us but from this interaction of basic needs and their fulfilment or damage we will form motivational goals that will either aim to fulfil or protect our basic needs. These will be manifested in the way we interact with the world. This is again essential for us to understand as these explain the heart, the soul, of motivation and how we, mostly unconsciously, choose to interact with the world around us.

4.4 Motivational Schemata

Humans will strive to fulfil these four basic needs, consciously or unconsciously, on a daily basis. We will therefore moderate and form our behaviours and our interaction with the environment in such a way as to conform with our own individual motivational schema based on the satisfaction and fulfilment (or protection) of our basic needs (see Fig. 4.2).

Motivational schemata are the instruments and methods that a person will develop through their lifetime to help satisfy their basic needs or to protect them. Within this theory exist two base schemata. On one hand the *approach schema* which is a result of a person striving to fulfil their basic needs. Through this striving and through satisfaction and fulfilment of these needs, a positive motivational schema will be laid down as positive memories and experiences, consciously but mostly unconsciously. On the other hand if a person strives to protect their basic needs this is known as an *avoidance schema*. The individual with an avoidance scheme will strive to protect their basic needs against danger, threats and potential damage. This draws on previous negative experiences of damaged basic needs and hence the individual will attempt to avoid this repetition (Grawe 2006). Research has shown that satisfaction of the basic needs in early childhood activates various patterns that influence the later behaviour of adults (Grawe 2006).

These schemata show that the interpretation of the basic needs and the motivation for the fulfilment of them are driven individually based on the whole history of experiences that each individual has been exposed to. This in turn will influence the interpretation of various contexts and lead to various avoidance or approach strategies and actions.

From these basic needs, therefore, develop various motivational goals. These are formed from the previous experiences of the satisfaction, or not, of the basic needs and the respective neuronal patterns in the brain. If the individual has been able, through their experiences, to develop positive motivational schemata then they will strive to fulfil all their basic needs and one will not be satisfied at the cost of another (Grawe 2006).

4.5   Motivational Systems and Personality Types

As we have shown, and as is supported by neuroscientific study, personal motivation is driven by the development of approach or avoidance schemes. The bipolar idea, which had been long established, that individual schemes operate along one dimension or that schemes balance each other out is no longer sustainable. Even though the approach and avoidance schemata operate as two distinct systems, they can stimulate independent neuronal substrates. This is, in part because of lateralisation, the separation of the hemispheres which have differing functions (which, however, are interdependent on each other). The left hemisphere deals more with positive emotions and hence will be more stimulated with the approach schemata and in the right hemisphere, the "sadder" hemisphere (McGilchrist 2009), the avoidance scheme is more likely to be observed.

These neuronal motivation systems can also be brought together with the standard theory in personality psychology—the Big Five Model which was first proposed by Tupes and Christal (1961) but independent sets of researchers have come up with similar findings (including: Costa and McCrae 1992). The Big Five Model, or Five Factor Model (FFM) has emerged as a robust model for measuring personality over the last 50 years (Digman 1990; Goldberg 1993; Saulsman 2004; Barrick and Mount 1991). The five factors are: openness, conscientiousness, extraversion, agreeableness and neuroticism. In the two areas of extraversion and neuroticism we can place the two poles of the motivational schemata.

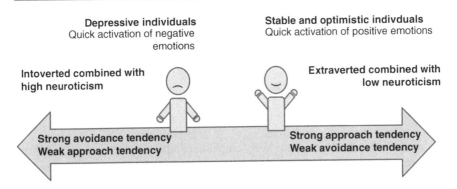

Fig. 4.3 Personality types and motivational systems

The dimensions of **Introversion / Extraversion** measure the interactivity of a person with their environment. With relation to the workplace, introverted workers are those that are generally passive members of a team and take on a more observational roles rather than taking action. Reflective, quiet and withdrawn are typical characteristics. They will avoid promoting themselves and are not seen as emotional-studies have shown that they can be very emotional but do not show this (Eysenck 1967; Eysenck and Eysenck 1985; Kumari et al. 2004). Extraverted workers in contrast enjoy company and are attracted to social groups and take an active role within them. They will actively look for interaction with co-workers and are seen in the workplace as talkative, social, enthusiastic and animated.

On the scales of introversion and extraversion there is also a correlation with avoidance or approach strategies. The more extraverted a person the more they will tend to implement approach strategies to satisfy their basic needs and are more able to activate positive emotions. Conversely introverted people will tend not to use approach strategies and positive emotions may be more difficult to activate.

Neuroticism represents the emotional stability of a person. Employees who have high levels of neuroticism will be often confronted with negative emotional states (and are often overwhelmed by these) and have many problems and these problems cause emotional turmoil. People with high neuroticism often feel insecure. People with low neuroticism are calm and balanced, they do not perceive many problems and are resistant to high emotional and stress situations.

With high levels of neuroticism there seems to be a strong correlation to avoidance strategies with regard to satisfaction of the basic needs. In contrast individuals with low neuroticism tend to show low levels of avoidance and low correlation to negative emotions.

If we tie these personality theories to the consistency model and motivational schemata we can see the complete cycle of interaction (see Fig. 4.3).

The influence of personality psychology is of particular relevance and importance for these approaches. Obviously putting people into two personality types is extremely simplified yet this allows us to illustrate a model that can be applied in a broader context and hence we should see its value as a pragmatic tool while

Fig. 4.4 Experience of congruence

understanding, as we have continually emphasised, that the background to and the variations of this will be different between each individual.

4.6   Consistency Theory Model

The consistency theory model is the combination of the four basic needs of humans and the resulting motivational schemata into an overlying general model. Consistency refers to the state of the underlying neuronal processes and the psychological states being in balance and in harmony (Grosse Holtforth et al. 2007). People will feel at their best when these basic needs are fulfilled and in harmony and this can be achieved through their own motivational schemata. The drive to fulfil, or protect, these basic needs is mostly driven unconsciously and this urge for fulfilment of these needs will be placed in order of priority in front of other specific individual needs. If a person can fulfil their basic needs then this can, and likely will be, acknowledged by the individual and hence further influence their motivational schemata. If these motivational schemata are in line with our perception of the world i.e. they are realistically able to lead to fulfilment of the basic needs, then we have congruence.

An employee has been working now for two years in a large corporation. Their work has been successful and they have been given increasingly more responsibility and autonomy. This the motivated employee has used to formulate higher and more challenging goals which they have achieved. This employee has therefore developed the wish to further their career with this organisation and has focused their efforts on this. After the last successful project a promotion was given to this employee.

Congruence is the link between current motivational goals and our experience of the world (Grawe 2006; Fig. 4.4):

Incongruence exists when this harmony is disturbed and comes in three forms (Grosse Holtforth et al. 2007):

1. **Approach incongruence**

   Neuronal formed tendencies give rise to a behaviour pattern that strives to fulfil the approach, achievement that is, of goals. If these are inhibited by avoidance then incongruence is the result, as this will block fulfilling or approaching one's basic needs.

   An employee would like to run a project independently, is however anxious about leading their own project and making their own decisions and taking more responsibility. This person therefore remains reluctantly and unhappily as an assistant in the project.

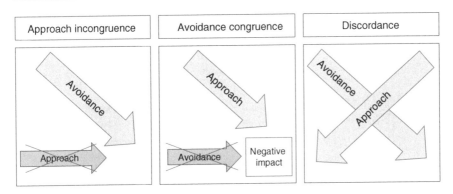

Fig. 4.5 Forms of incongruence

2. **Avoidance incongruence**

   If strongly formed approach tendencies override inhibition, avoidance, strategies that is, then there will be no protection against disappointment if the needs cannot be fulfilled. If this is then the case then we have avoidance incongruence.

   After a number of years in training and engaging on various projects the employee now feels less anxious about taking on a project and takes over the lead in a major project. However, the goals were not achieved and the project is unsuccessful.

3. **Discordance**

   Approach and avoidance tendencies are activated and active at the same time and block each other. This leads to neither the approach nor the avoidance strategy being fulfilled. This is a motivational conflict.

   In this case the employee cannot decide and is therefore in an internal conflict. Senior management has offered this employee a position in a foreign subsidiary. The employee, on one hand, is happy about the offer and the new chances but, on the other hand, afraid to the same extent of the potential problems and challenges.

   These three forms of incongruencies (see Fig. 4.5) lead to inconsistency. If no strategies are developed to overcome this then this will lead to enduring negative emotions and states (Grawe 2006). Fig 4.6 is a diagrammatic representation of the Consistency Theory Model.

   The Consistency Theory Model is hence the sum of basic needs, motivational schemata and the feedback from the external world. It explains how the basic needs are formed but importantly how these are manifested onto our motivational goals which are based on our experience of the world and the neuronal networks and associations we have built over our life. These are continually interacting with each other and continually feeding our internal feedback system. These will then be transposed onto our interactions, our way of interacting and behaving in the world that we interact with. Specifically, within the context of this book, the importance is how we interact with the business world and how in leadership and business contexts this is manifested. As we can see from the Consistency Theory Model the basic needs lie at the heart of this and from this we can draw the motivational

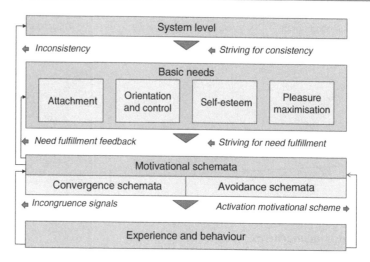

Fig. 4.6 Consistency theory model (Grawe 2006)

schemata of approach or avoidance. We will discuss this in Chap. 5 with respect to various organisational, personnel development tools and leadership concepts. In Chap. 6 we will also give a model (ACTIVE model) of how you can use this in a non-therapeutic corporate context (which is our ultimate goal).

4.7   Application in Neuropsychotherapy

The Consistency Theory Model was developed with neuropsychotherapy in mind and in therapeutic contexts there are two questionnaires designed to gather information on patient's motivational schemata and the manifestations of their approach and avoidance schemata. These were developed by Grawe and Grosse Holtforth. Here a short overview:

1. Questionnaire for analysis of motivational schemata (FAMOS) (Holtforth and Grawe 2000)

   The **Questionnaire for analysis of motivational schemata (FAMOS)** is a questionnaire that has been developed in the German-speaking area for use in assessing patients in therapeutic settings. The questionnaire collects data and measures the intensity of experience and behaviour in relation to their approach and avoidance schemata.

2. Incongruence questionnaire (INK) (Holtforth and Grawe 2003)

   The **Incongruence questionnaire** builds on the analysis of motivational schemata and further development. This is integrated in an incongruence questionnaire to ascertain the intensity of the approach and avoidance goals to measure the degree of completion of these goals. This therefore measures the difference between a personal goals and the reality. This is used to plan the therapy and the evaluation in clinical settings.

The use of these questionnaires is focused on therapeutic interventions and is a tool to help develop strategies and goals for the therapy. These therefore have little relevance, as they stand, for analysis of leadership styles and for use in organisations. In addition it is not the role of organisations to treat psychologically sick individuals. Nevertheless the principle of these questionnaires provides a basis that can be applied to business administration in a modified form as they can show various facets and faces of basic needs and motivational schemata.

4.8 Summary

- Human beings strive to fulfil and satisfy their **basic needs** as supported by neuroscientific theory and this can be seen in forms of **congruence**. The four basic needs are:
  - **Attachment:** the building of a positive relationship, and bonding, to an attachment person.
  - **Orientation and control:** to be able to orientate oneself in the world and the environment and be able to exert influence over the personal environment and context.
  - **Self-esteem protection and development:** the need to build and develop a self-image and self worth.
  - **Pleasure maximisation and pain avoidance:** the striving for pleasurable states.
- The inability to satisfy one or more basic needs is known as **incongruence.** This will per se mean that the individual will be unable to achieve their goals in their context.
- **Consistency** is, on the other hand, the harmony between the environment and context and the fulfilment of an individual's basic needs.
- **Motivational schemata** are the individual interpretation of motives and drives to achieve their goals in the current context. Here we can differentiate between **approach** schemata and **avoidance** schemata.
  - Approach is the state of an individual actively pursuing the fulfilment of their basic needs.
  - Avoidance is the state of an individual protecting their basic needs in place of striving to fulfil and increase them.

Organisational and Personnel Development Tools in the Neuroscience Spotlight

5

In this chapter we will look into specific instruments and theories from organisational and personnel development and leadership concepts and look at these through the spectacles of neuroscience and the four basic needs. This will enable us to evaluate these current approaches from a neuroscientific view and therefore to highlight their effects on personnel and the environment from a viewpoint of the brain and the four basic needs.

Objectives

- Understand the neural basis of the basic needs
- Understand how organisational development can impact each of the four basic needs
- Understand how leadership concepts can impact each of the four basic needs

5.1 Introduction

In this chapter we aim to go into the practical understanding of neuroscience in the workplace. We will use the model of the four basic needs as an overriding model. We use this, as we mentioned in the introduction to this book, because these are at the base of human interaction and of the brain's interaction with the environment. Creating consistency and congruence here will enable employees to fulfil their true potential and hence the business to perform at its maximum also.

In the following pages we take various organisational and personal developmental tools and place these under the neuroscience spotlight. This will highlight what each tool's strengths are and specifically which neural systems each tool will target. This will also explain why some of these tools (assuming they have been well implemented) will work better for some employees than others. It is because each tool will target different underlying neural networks. Depending on the emotional basic needs of the employees and their underlying motivational schema (as outlined in

A. Ghadiri et al., *Neuroleadership*, Management for Professionals,
DOI 10.1007/978-3-642-30165-0_5, © Springer-Verlag Berlin Heidelberg 2012

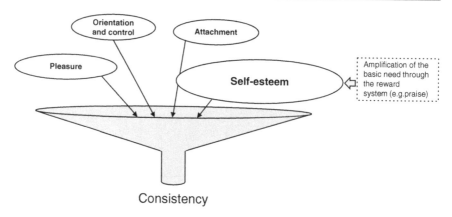

Fig. 5.1 Reward system and consistency

chapter 4)—and respective neuronal networks—each employee will respond differently to each tool.

Every employee has developed, over years, their lifetime indeed, specific and general reward systems which will include factors such as status, financial reward, free time, praise, etc. These reward systems will be very individual and formed by previous experiences with previous management forms and systems. These will have helped to form and fulfil basic needs—or not. Indeed these experiences may have caused damage and hence an employee may have developed an avoidance motivational schema.

We can also picture this fulfilment of a basic need as a reward amplifier – if there is strong desire for self-esteem then fulfilling, this in part, will have disproportionate effect on reward. In Fig. 5.1 we can see a situation in which an employee is very sensitive to praise and this leads to a particular need for fulfilment of the basic need of self-esteem.

5.2   The Effect of Personnel and Organisational Approaches

Before we look at the tools themselves we will first review the four basic needs and think of them in the context of interaction in the workplace. This is the heart of neuroleadership—understanding the core human drives and their respective neuronally linked circuits and from this be able to generate ways of interacting with employees that will best activate their personal neuronal circuits.

We will illustrate the specific needs and neuronal processes that each will activate and what considerations need to be taken by leadership teams in deciding to implement and approach these in their specific context. We are here therefore projecting these neuroscientific findings into a concrete working environment.[1]

---

[1] We should note that we have not entered into a cultural discussion and cultural influences here. Obviously there will be strong cultural influences.

Fig. 5.2 Positive effect of oxytocin

(1) Activating the basic need for attachment

Intensive social interaction leads to the release of the "attachment" hormone oxytocin (see Sect. 4.2.1). This will help build trust and help bonding with a person or group of people (Kosfeld et al. 2005; Baumgartner et al. 2008).

The assumption is that leadership forms that involve a higher interaction between leaders and their employees help to promote the basic need of attachment (which includes bonding). In addition organisational development instruments that foresee collaborative working patterns can, through the increased interaction with and between people, lead to positive relationships being formed. We noted in Sect. 4.2.1 the influence of oxytocin and in a simplified version of this we can see oxytocin as the trust hormone. There are however a number of criteria that need to be met for trust to be present:

- Trust is reciprocal, trust must be given not earned (Salamon & Robinson 2008; Van Den Bos et al. 2009)
- Interests must be aligned (Boudreau et al. 2009; Burnham 2000)
- Fear must be low (Ross 2011; Williams 2007)
- Actions and behaviour strengthen trust or can breach it (Hurley 2006; Barclay 2006)

It is also important to note that mistrust activates the amygdala and can be seen as threat activation in the brain (Pillay 2009; Rock 2009). This is the classic "friend or foe" construct that we seem to be inherently born with. Simply trust is a form of friendship and bonding, whereas mistrust is linked with threat and fear. This can give rise to unconstructive, aggressive and protective behaviours but also be linked with the brain functioning we described in Sect. 2.7.2 whereby fear distorts brain functioning and inhibits cognitive power, collaboration and cooperation and hence creativity while giving a negative bias to the environment.

Further influences on this will be the general atmosphere and the ability of employees to build relationships amongst themselves and with leaders. Some of these may be a little soft and elusive—it is hard to describe the chemistry that connects some people more strongly to others. This said much of this is linked to having a trusting environment that we have just spoken about. By understanding this, and focusing on this, leaders will be able to create a stronger context for the formation of stronger relationships (Fig. 5.2).

(2) Activating the basic need for orientation and control

We spoke in Sect. 4.2.2 of the need for orientation and control. This is potentially underestimated in leadership contexts: the view of Taylor (see Sect. 5.5.1) is still embedded in companies today—that of not informing employees of processes or indeed of crucial decisions within the company. Insecurity and lack of

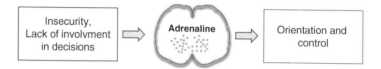

Fig. 5.3 Negative effect of adrenaline

involvement in decisions over our personal future and work contexts can lead to a stress reaction and the release of adrenaline (Zink et al. 2008).

Leaders who form goals without involving the employees and who do not offer transparency will also have a negative impact on the basic need for orientation and control. Leaders can approach this in two ways. Firstly by giving more orientation—that means giving information (we noted in Sect. 2.5.2 that information can also function as secondary reward). Even when the information is negative, this is likely to be better than no information. Ambiguity and lack of information, as we noted above, activates the amygdala—also our fear centres. Information even if negative can at least give more orientation. It will also drive trust in organisations. Secondly orientation and control can be stimulated in working contexts by allowing more personal control over the environment. These may be small things such as being able to personalize the workplace but also in defining, to some extent, working times. This basic need will be better fulfilled when employees have room and space to either control or influence the actions, goals and work environment which will lead to avoiding unnecessary stress situations for employees (Fig. 5.3).

(3) Activating the basic need for self-esteem and its protection and development

Any situation that aims to criticise or praise a person has the potential to damage, or feed, the basic need for self-esteem. Situations such as feedback and performance reviews, whereby an employee is criticized by a more senior person, subjectively, can lead to the release of cortisol if an employee feels their status is threatened (Korsten et al. 2007; Hüther 2009). Performance reviews will therefore strongly influence the basic need for self-esteem.

Leaders and management therefore need to be sensitive to the differing ways and approaches of dealing with employees, how they can be constructive and how leaders can look to develop each of their employees. This means that a leader or manager in these situations needs to be able to engage the employee in a respectful way and to be able to bring their skills and talent to the forefront of a conversation. The "hamburger" system of feedback is also a powerful method. The bread is the positives the meat is the negative, the areas to be improved. However, it is essential to start with the positives and to end with the positives. The "meat" also needs to be defined in an understanding and non-personal away. By non-personal we mean in a way so as to not threaten the whole individual themselves but rather a simple action or act. This is a solid method for feedback.

Feedback should also not be left to the regular formal performance review but should be a part of daily business (feedback also serves to feed the basic need of

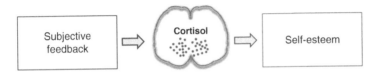

Fig. 5.4 Negative effects of cortisol

orientation and control). Daily interactions and praise and encouragement will help employees to understand their self-esteem and build their performance. This, we stress again, must be done in a respectful and positive way. This will be easier if the attachment and bonding levels (basic need for attachment) are high (Fig. 5.4).

(4) Activation of the basic need for pleasure and pain avoidance

Pleasure can come in many forms but in business contexts this is usually left to chance. Winning a big contract, successfully completing a challenging task, and so on and so forth. These will indeed lead to the release of dopamine which will lead to a feeling of satisfaction and happiness which in turn will lead to further motivation. Leaders should therefore focus on increasing reward of employees in different ways. We noted that attachment, bonding and self-esteem all can stimulate feelings of reward (this is where the basic needs overlap strongly). Similarly our primary rewards, as we noted in Sect. 2.5.2, stimulate the reward system. Included in primary rewards are simple things like food and drink. A team meal can hence increase pleasure but also increase attachment and bonding. Moreover tasks that are at the level and skills of the employees and that give an inherent free room to solve them will also strengthen the feelings of reward.

Leaders therefore should think of how employees can be rewarded or have rewarding experiences at work, whether it be through praise, through small presents or, successful task completion or increased status. These will all stimulate the reward system, positive feelings and also help form good habits and positive learning experiences (Fig. 5.5).

5.3   Instruments of Personnel and Organisational Development

Here we will look at some standard instruments of organisational development that are designed to improve the working atmosphere and the motivation and efficiency of employees. These areas by their nature will have an overlap with personnel development which focuses on developing the skills and competencies of employees. Many organisational tools can also have an impact on personnel development by, for example, increasing the responsibility of an employee. Indeed organisational development and personnel development should be so designed as to complement each other. We have chosen six well-known models here for our neuroscientific analysis. Our purpose here is not to give new models but to show these standard models in a new light and shed the understanding of neuroleadership on these and what they do and do not do for the brain of the employee. The thought

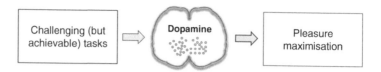

Fig. 5.5 Positive effects of dopamine

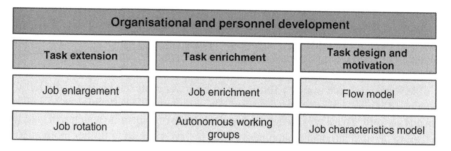

Fig. 5.6 A selection of organisational and personnel development instruments

process of considering the four basic needs is the core of our approach. Figure 5.6 lists the six models we have chosen.

5.3.1   Job Enlargement

Job enlargement is, as the name suggests, the expansion of a person's job or function. In this context, however, it does not mean increasing the workload but rather increasing the variety of tasks of an individual. The goal is to provide a wider variety and to counteract monotonous work (Olfert 2010; Reif and Schoderbek 1966). Figure 5.7 represents this diagrammatically (see Fig. 5.7).

5.3.1.1 Evaluation

From a neuroscientific perspective job enlargement is a good way to help satisfy the basic need of increasing *self-esteem*. In increasing an individual's feeling of self worth and making a person's work more worthwhile and relevant. As this does not increase the responsibility (and hence uncertainty and fear of failure or increase in pressure) this is a good approach to boost motivational schemata.

Whether job enlargement will also increase the basic need for *orientation and control* is heavily debated currently. This increase in the number of tasks may bring more variety but this may not involve more control or orientation—indeed arguably it will lower this as more tasks can decrease our overview. Herzberg in Germany criticised this heavily by noting: nothing + nothing = nothing (Herzberg 2003). This is true only if the type of work done does not increase the control or orientation. So the model is not such to be criticized as the definition of the tasks—it is the type of task that increases orientation and control.

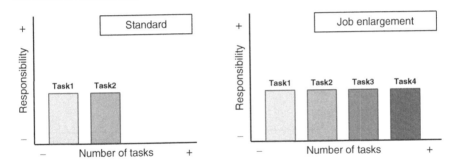

Fig. 5.7 Job enlargement

The basic need of *attachment* will also not necessarily be increased with job enlargement as a concept. Again this is dependent on the task that is used to enlarge a job. If the task involves more interaction then this will potentially lead to increased social interaction positive experiences and increased attachment and bonding.

The basic need for *pleasure maximisation* would be increased with job enlargement as variety in itself will stimulate the brain more and lead to an increase in satisfaction. There is however again a dependence on the type of task. If new tasks are given that are not within an individual's qualifications and skills and competencies, this will increase their anxiety. However, a key defining feature of job enlargement is the expansion of tasks within an individual's skills and competencies and hence increased opportunities to fulfil tasks.

We can therefore see that job enlargement has the ability to fulfil at least some of the basic needs and hence to increase the level of satisfaction in the job. We do note that the implementation of one organisational change will not lead to an immediate shift in the whole satisfaction of the basic needs of the entire workforce—this is an illusion. Some may find the increased number of tasks particularly stimulating. Others may initially feel a sense of anxiety as their feeling of security may be threatened mildly. This highlights the individual basic needs of each employee (see Chap. 6 for individual implementation). As with all the tools we speak about here care and common sense are needed in its implementation. The same applies to the tasks given which will be limited and defined by the type of work and business we are in.

5.3.2   Job Rotation

Job rotation, as the name suggests, is the rotation, changing of jobs, within an organisation. Job rotation should be a planned and organised process (sporadic and unstructured implementations backfire and lead to insecurity and a feeling of unfairness in an organisation). Job rotation should include changing to jobs that involve similar skills and competencies and responsibilities remain at a similar level to the previous job (Schultz and Schultz 2009) (see Fig. 5.8). This can be

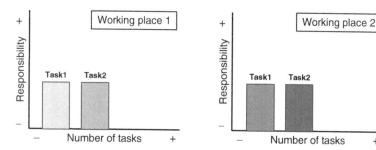

Fig. 5.8 Job rotation

changing jobs within an organisation, changing to a different team in a large organisation, changing to a similar role in a different department or in the case of international organisations changing to a similar role in a different country. This again is to increase the variety and break the monotony of a specific job. The concept of job rotation would however, envisage the employee coming back to their original job after a defined period of time.

Job rotation is particularly effective in dealing with and avoiding repetitive nature of jobs but also to challenge and improve the range of skills and competencies of employees. In addition it can also help, in large organisations to increase the social network and to increase the understanding of the business as a whole. It is therefore not just to combat monotony but also to boost ability, experience and hence quality.

5.3.2.1 Evaluation

Job rotation allows employees to take on a different role while keeping the responsibility similar or the same. This means there is less danger of being over challenged in comparison to job enlargement which by its nature, increasing tasks, can lead to over challenge. New environments and activities in different contexts can increase the basic need for pleasure maximisation. The basic need for *self-esteem* can also be increased in this context.

The basic need for *attachment* is particularly positively influenced, as a new environment will also mean that there will be new bonds formed. If it is in the context of a rob rotation scheme, whereby the job rotation is temporary, this will also positively influence this (changing jobs can also cause a stress reaction but is much less likely in a certain given time frame as the old bonds and attachments are not lost). The new social interactions will increase attachment. However, as we mentioned in Sect. 4.1.1 those who have avoidant attachment models will be difficult to satisfy. The basic need for *orientation and control* will not be approached in a job rotation context.

There are numerous other positive knock-on effect within job rotation. It enables bonding and forming relationships in different parts of an organisation. This is particularly important for larger organisations where employees can lose the over-view and the connections to other parts of organisation. It will also enable an

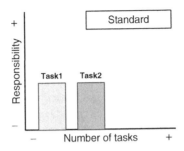 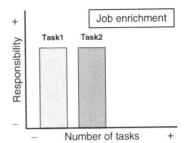

Fig. 5.9 Job enrichment

understanding of the business in different forms (and in international corporations in different countries).

Other forms of this may involve taking a stint in a different department—this is not a pure job rotation principle but will help understand different parts of the organisation while increasing variety and bonding and networking in different parts.

As we mentioned earlier it is, however, important that job rotation programmes are well planned. This avoids disruption and does not challenge the basic need of orientation and control—indeed this can increase this if well designed. Also the clarity will provide a stable structure and make it clear who and how and when and for how long. This will also make it a fair system and not a system that may be perceived to help a few select individuals.

5.3.3 Job Enrichment

Job enrichment is the increase of a person's responsibilities within a job. In contrast to job enlargement which involves increasing the tasks but not the responsibly or scope, job enrichment is the increase in responsibility and scope and relevant free room (Cunningham and Eberle 1990). This may involve taking on new tasks but can just as easily be increased responsibility for the same task (see Fig. 5.9). This can again reduce the monotony of the work and increase the variation and interest be stimulated (Mohr and Zoghi 2006). Pfeiffer noted the following as elements for job enrichment in industrial contexts (Pfeiffer et al. 1977):

- An employee prepares their machine themselves and ensure all the material and tools are ready and in functioning order.
- The production control is done independently by the employee and any corrections made.
- The working times and hours are individually decided by the employee.

5.3.3.1 Evaluation

In comparison to the other two mentioned already, job enrichment has its largest influence on the basic need for *orientation and control*. With an enlarged field of responsibility the individual will consequently have more room to influence their own particular environmental and way of working.

Additionally through increased activities and free room this can also activate the basic need for *self-esteem*. This increased freedom and responsibility is also a strong message from leaders that they are valued and trusted. The increased extension of activities also has the potential to increase the interaction with the environment and that means increased interaction with other employees and parts of an organisation. This in turn may have a positive impact on the basic need for *attachment*. This is, however, dependant on the type of tasks and the role within a particular type of organisation. Increased ability to produce tools in an industrial context may not impact this but in a financial service sector where increased responsibility may mean increased interaction in a project team, it will.

As in the previous examples it is important to note that the way and form of the job enrichment will have varying degrees of impact on varying basic needs. This is dependant on the type and role and also of the type of organisation and the sector the organisation is active in. In addition as we have continually stressed different people may react in different ways to job enrichment depending on their own needs and perceptions of the world.

5.3.4   Autonomous Work Groups

When job enrichment is not simply focused on an individual but on teams, for example, then we speak of autonomous work groups (Roth 1999). These are small groups of employees, generally between three and ten, who work together on a closed function. This may mean, however, that there be substantial changes in the working environment.

The level of autonomy may be larger or smaller depending on the tasks, the corporation and how this has been organised. The best–known categorisation of this is by Gullowsen who defined the following characteristics (Gullowsen 1972):

1. The group can influence their goals
   a. With respect to quality
   b. With respect to quantity
2. Within certain guidelines the group can define
   a. Where they work
   b. When they work
   c. What additional activities they do
3. The group can decide on the production methods
4. The group defines the internal task allocation
5. The group decides who belongs to the group
6. The group decides leadership issues of
   a. Whether they need a manager for internal issues and who this is
   b. Whether they would like to have a manager/supervisor for the regulation of guidelines

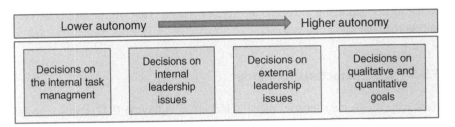

Fig. 5.10 Levels of autonomy in autonomous work groups

The implementation of this is in practice very varied. Whereas points 4, 5 and 6a are often applied points 1a, 1b and 6b are seldom seen (Fig. 5.10).

An example of autonomous working groups is that of the Volvo production facility in the Swedish town of Uddevalla. From 1989 the production was shifted to a more autonomous group production mode. In place of an assembly line process the assembly was given to teams of eight who each produced four cars a day. Each group was given relative autonomy as to how to do this and the hierarchies were kept flat. In each group there was careful mix of young and old and also of women. This led to a very positive and productive working environment (Turner and Sandberg 1996).

SEMCO in Brazil is another well-known case of a democratic company working strongly with autonomous teams (Semler 2006; Semler et al. 1998; Vanderburg 2004; Semler 1994) *as is W. L. Gore & Associates* (Manz et al. 2009).

5.3.4.1 Evaluation

Autonomous working groups form a strong basis for the satisfaction and fulfilment of the basic needs. A key difference to other methods mentioned above is that these draw in a whole group of individuals. In this constellation a group of individuals come together to decide and define various characteristics of their working environment, way of interacting and way of organising their work. Within these working groups, various groups of individuals come together and collect information and exchange experiences—this fulfils the basic need of *attachment*. As there is autonomy of the work group this is likely to generate a strong feeling of belonging and attachment and this also drives loyalty.

As the group, not the individual, decides on part of their goals, methods and ways of interacting and working there is a high level of autonomy and self control and each individual can contribute to this process. This will lead to a high level of satisfaction of the basic need of *orientation and control.*

Within this group as the group decides on their own goals and how they will approach this and the group decides on the input of the individuals we can assume that the group will target goals within their skills and competencies and in a field that they gain some satisfaction out of. This in turn will mean that the likelihood of satisfying the need for *pleasure* is greatly increased, as the roles will be defined according to personal preferences but in understanding of the group's goals.

As the group allows each individual to give their input each person will be taken more seriously and will not have a passive role in the formation of the goals and in taking orders and being a passive member of a team. This will in turn positively impact the feelings of *self-esteem*.

5.3.5 Job Characteristics Model

Hackmann's job characteristics model (Hackmann and Suttle 1977) focuses on the specific job, the tasks involves, how they are put together and how this influences the whole job. This works from the belief that optimal task organisation leads to higher employee satisfaction through engaging the employee fully and creating a better overview. Optimal definition of a task is defined using the following.

- **Skill variety**: the task should have some inherent variety within it so that employees can use different competencies and different facets of their skills.
- **Task identity**: an employee should be able to see the task as more complete and be more instrumental in forming a complete task rather than an individual step of a larger task.
- **Task significance:** the task should be an important part of the whole and that will enable the employee to be a part of something bigger and feel they are contributing to something valuable.
- **Task autonomy:** the employee should be given as much free room as possible to complete their task independently and the necessary inherent preparation and planning.
- **Task feedback:** the employee needs direct feedback on the success and satisfaction of their work and on how well they have achieved their tasks.

The five dimensions of the task organisation will have varying psychological impacts on each employee. This will also be different according to the development of the individual employee and each dimension will respectively have a different effect. Fig 5.11 diagrammatically represents the relationships here.

5.3.5.1 Evaluation

The job characteristics model has the potential to fulfil all basic needs. The variety of tasks and the significance of the tasks will lead to satisfying the need for *self-esteem*. The variety will also enable the employee to develop their skills and there will be a suitable amount of challenge and this has the potential to satisfy the *pleasure* need by making the tasks and work more enjoyable. Through the principle of task autonomy the employees will be able to take control of the tasks and work on it independently and this will help to fulfil the basic need for *orientation and control*.

A core principle of the job characteristics model is that of the need for growth and this is approached through the task feedback which enables regular and consistent opportunities to improve their skills and competencies and their ability to complete tasks to or above the standards required. This, however, requires consistent feedback with the leader and with others in the environment and this contact and mutual feedback process and interaction will therefore build on the basic need for *attachment*. The leader will be consistently involved with helping the

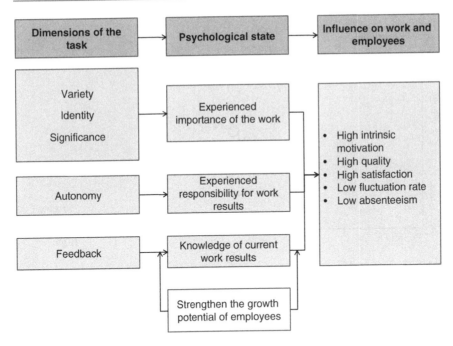

Fig. 5.11 Job-characteristics model

individual to become better and grow and this is a situation which has the potential for strong relationships to be built.

Applying job characteristics may be a challenge in the workplace—the model itself gives no direct recommendation on how to implement it. And it by default would need jobs and tasks that have an inherent flexibility in arranging and organising and defining the tasks. There is also a danger that this over focus on tasks could lead to a focus on detail and never-ending task design without moving forward. Nevertheless the model has the ability to satisfy the basic needs and thought should be given as to how it could be refined to any business.

5.3.6 Flow

The concept of flow was first put forward by Mihaly Csikszentmihalyi (Csikszentmihalyi 1991) who, in his research into creativity, encountered artists who would get so involved in their work that they become totally disengaged from the world. They moved into a state where they were completely involved, when time was distorted and when they even lost sense of when to eat, drink and sleep. More importantly for us is that in this state their was a sense of satisfaction and his initial book "Flow" is subtitled "the psychology of optimal experience". It is in that sense the concept of achieving happiness because if you are in a state of flow you will be inherently satisfied and happy. Indeed he uses the term "autotelic" which

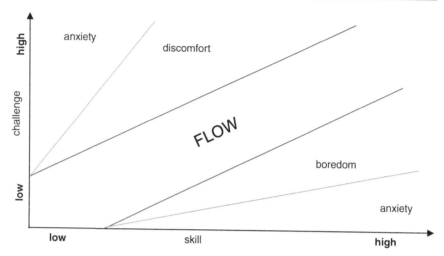

Fig. 5.12 Flow model

states that the job, or task, then becomes a self-fulfilling prophecy i.e. that it is inherently enjoyable and hence motivating and hence pleasurable which in turn feeds further motivation.

Csikszentmihalyi defined a number of characteristics that need to be in place for flow to occur and in the workplace one key defining characteristics is the balance of challenge and skill. Too much challenge for an individual and this individual will feel anxious or become stressed. Too little challenge for a person's skill set and this will lead to boredom (see Fig. 5.12).

Flow is moreover an emotional state and this will be influenced by various factors in the workplace. Csikszentmihalyi defined the following characteristics that need to be in place for flow to occur:

- There must be clear goal which gives direction and structure.
- There must be a balance between challenge and skills. See above.
- There must be clear and immediate feedback.

An interesting note here is that if we look at computer games and their ability to be addictive and activate certain states, we can actually see that they fulfil all the above criteria. Each game has a clear goal. Through the structure of computer games of moving from easy to higher levels of difficulty they allow each player to get to a state of optimal level between challenge and personal skills. But in addition computer games also give clear and immediate feedback. This is interesting because these elements can also be implemented relatively simply in the workplace and this will therefore influence the ability of workers to get into this positive and enjoyably emotional state which is maybe per se the definition of motivation itself but certainly of productivity. This can be done in the workplace through the following:

- Employees should have clear goals, ideally individual goals that have been mutually defined.

- Leaders will need to give employees consistent, regular, constructive and positive feedback of their work.
- Employees should be given tasks that have the prerequisite amount of challenge based on their skills and competencies.
- The employee should have some influence on the direction and way of solving the task given.
- In times of change employees should be allowed to flexibly change their time management.

5.3.6.1 Evaluation

By taking the flow model into consideration leaders will enable employees to experience the workplace and the tasks as positive experiences. Indeed the theory of flow is considered an experience for happiness and optimal experience of life. In his book Csikszentmihalyi gives many examples from the workplace and how workers can tap into flow to have a thoroughly engaging and rewarding experience at work. This is easy to underestimate but he has a fundamental argument and that is our experience of the world is what drives our happiness. From a neuroscientific perspective, which we approach here, and the basic needs we can see the following:

The basic need of *attachment* will be allowed to develop through the close interaction with the leader who through the model will be giving regular feedback and this will allow the closer bonding and building of relationships.

The basic need of *orientation and control* is a key element of flow, as it requires clear, immediate feedback, this gives clear orientation. Furthermore it defines that the challenge and competencies must be aligned which leads to being in control of tasks and avoiding the anxiety and stress of over-challenge.

The state of flow itself is by definition a pleasurable state and the concept of optimal experience suggests, as it is indeed, that we are talking about increasing our experience of life and fulfilling our basic need for *pleasure*.

By the same token we can see that this state of optimal experience is a fulfilling and rewarding experience for an employee. The balance of challenge and competencies will mean that the individual will be able to achieve their goals but this achievement will be rewarding as it is optimally balanced with their skills. This will therefore not only be a rewarding experience but also feed the *self-esteem* the self worth and value that a person experiences.

Though the state of flow may seem at times a little esoteric it is not, this happens to many of us at many times, it is a state that we all have experienced and the implementation will require some thought but mostly a lot of intuition and sensitivity to the given situation. But many of the concepts, that of regular feedback, for example, may be easier to implement than many assume and the rewards may also potentially be greater than many can predict.

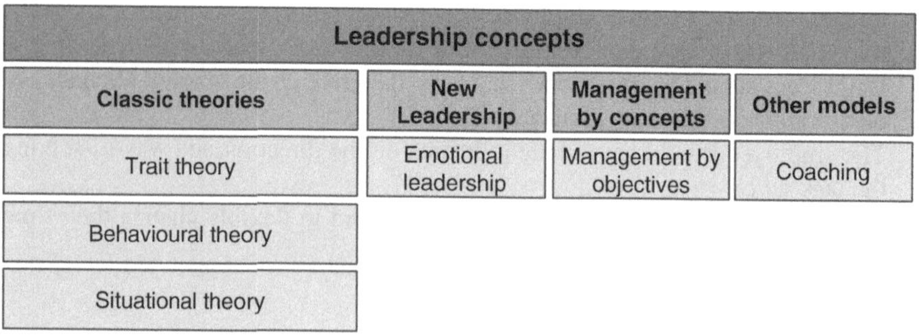

Leadership concepts			
Classic theories	**New Leadership**	**Management by concepts**	**Other models**
Trait theory	Emotional leadership	Management by objectives	Coaching
Behavioural theory			
Situational theory			

Fig. 5.13 Selected leadership concepts

5.4   Leadership Concepts

The process of leadership looks into how the balance of influencing factors between employee and leaders play together to influence the behaviours and actions of the employees and respective effectiveness in fulfilling the goals of the organisation. The boundaries between leadership theories and concepts are overlapping and hence we will speak of leadership concepts.

Trait theory, behavioural theory and situational theory are the historical roots of the development of leadership theory. Trait theory places the traits of the leader in the centre of attention and this is the key for leadership success. Behavioural theory works from the basis that it is the behaviours and not traits of leaders that influence their employees and resultant success. Situational theory takes this one step further and states that each situation will require different ways of leading. In more modern theories there is, for example in emotional leadership, a focus on emotions whereas "management by" concepts give sets of guidelines to lead better in given contexts. Further developments in this have taken on a broader approach such as coaching models for leadership. We will put the leadership concepts in Fig. 5.13 under the neuroscience spotlight.

5.4.1   Trait Theory

Trait leadership is one of the oldest theories in leadership and has its roots going back to the start of the 1900s and particularly the work of Gordon Allport (Allport 1961). This is tightly linked to personality psychology and the host of measures and tests that have been developed over the years and continue to be developed. Trait theory looks into the personality, the psyche, of leaders as individuals and measures various aspects of this. Current psychometric testing aims to define the specific traits that can be scientifically correlated to leadership success or to various factors such as creativity, derailment or emotional intelligence. In such, trait theory does not look at the working environment or context but is based on the belief that the traits of the leaders will define the success of a corporation. There have been a

Fig. 5.14 Traits of successful leaders

plethora of propositions as to what traits can or should be measured, including the big five we mentioned in Sect. 4.3. There is some consensus and empirical research to support the following six traits (Northouse 2008) (see Fig. 5.14):

- **Intelligence:** Defines verbal ability, decision making ability and arguing faculties that give rise to a clear mind and focused attention and problem solving ability. This is related, but not exclusively, to the actual IQ score. Though it needs to be said that IQ is consistently one of the highest correlates in leadership success. It is also important that the leaders are able to have and process knowledge about the job, sector or field of operation and use this to effect (in this sense this is not IQ as this measures cognitive abilities and not knowledge).
- **Confidence:** Leaders with confidence are able to make decisions and to stick with them: they are able to lead with clarity and without regret. This in turn is acknowledged and accepted by their employees and can help create a secure environment and impression of the leader and corporation.
- **Charisma:** Charisma has been ascribed to many leadership functions and, specifically, the impact of leadership. Specifically charismatic leaders can impart a sense of direction and motivate followers who are willing to be lead. Particularly when clear visions and clear goals are needed, charismatic leaders have powerful abilities to form and generate these visions and have a strong will to follow these goals and visions. Hoffman in 2011 (Hoffman et al. 2011) noted a very strong correlation to leadership effectiveness.
- **Determination:** Leaders will need to show focus and problem solving ability but importantly they will need to stand strong in conflict and in periods of criticism. To follow their goals and visions they will need to have the determination to put these into action against negativity, adversity and opposition.
- **Sociability:** Leaders need to be able to deal in a network of people and their interactions and problems and conflicts. To be able to solve these conflicts and to convince, persuade and solve personal problems well and with diplomacy they will need to have strong interpersonal skills. This enables the cooperative and collaborative working environment that for most corporations is a prerequisite for success.
- **Integrity:** Integrity is meant here in the context of the leadership relationship with employees meaning that the leader is reliable and honest to their employees. This will show itself in taking responsibility for the team and being transparent

about the corporation's activities. This is also a key driver for developing loyalty to the leader and the corporation.

5.4.1.1 Evaluation

Many elements in trait theory and the traits noted above show potential for fulfilling the basic need of *attachment* as the social skills and communication show a building of a strong base that enables powerful social and honest integrity which is the basis for forming relationships.

Other basic needs do not seem to be explicitly and clearly approached. However clarity and determination suggest an element of orientation that is necessary for the basic need of *control and orientation*. Social skills in themselves will be able to activate the *pleasure maximisation* as elements such as praise and limited conflicts can directly influence the pleasure of the working environment. The fulfilment of the basic needs will therefore be strongly dependant on the individual as they do not follow explicitly from the traits themselves.

5.4.2 Behavioural Theory

Behavioural theories explain the success of leadership through the ability of leaders to apply suitable behaviours. This came forth from criticisms of trait theory and aimed to explain leadership styles as sets of behaviours. From this sprung forth the managerial grid model (Blake and Mouton 1964) plotting on one axis the concern for production or goal achievement and on the other axis the concern for people. This based on two basic dimensions of leadership:

- **People centric leadership style:** the behaviours of the leader are focused on people, on the employee. They ensure that they feel comfortable and the leaders will support them and take their opinions and feelings into consideration.
- **Task centric leadership style:** the leader will focus on the tasks and the achievement of goals and this is the centre of their attention.

The challenge for leaders is to balance the care for people with achieving goals: "The best leaders get the job done and care about others in the process".

The following grid defined the various leadership styles (see Fig. 5.15):

- Low task/high people = country club style
- High task/high people = team style
- High task/low people = produce or perish style
- Low task/low people = impoverished
- Middle people/middle task = middle of the road

In addition behavioural theory takes into account how the leader involves employees in the decision making process and defined two basic types for this:

- **Participative leadership:** Employees will be involved in the decision-making processes and can therefore jointly help define the goals.
- **Autocratic leadership:** The leader defines the goals independently and gives strict instructions on how to achieve the goals.

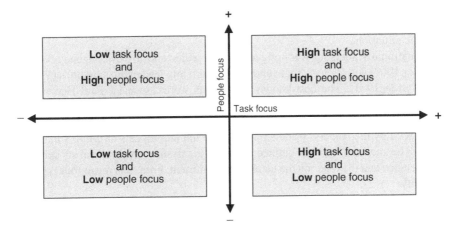

Fig. 5.15 Dimensions of leadership behaviour

5.4.2.1 Evaluation

The degree of positive impact on the basic needs of employees will be directly dependant on the style of leading that a leader uses and how these are combined. A high task centricity combined with a low people centricity and autocratic leadership will negatively impact the basic needs. We will therefore explore the potential impact on the basic needs from the combination of a people centric leadership style combined with participative leadership.

With a people centric leadership style the leader takes into consideration the employees and helps them solve their problems and takes their issues seriously: this will lead to a positive influence on the basic need for *attachment* as this will enable a closer relationship through mutual trust and consideration. Involving employees in the decision making process will help fulfil the basic need for *orientation and control* as they will be able to exert control over the work environment.

Though a direct impact on pleasure and self-esteem is not to be seen there is a clear indirect link to *self-esteem*. This as in the context of a participative leadership style the employees will be able to give their ideas and this is seen as a sign of trust and value of the opinions of employees. The dynamics of the team will define how impactful this actually is. This in itself could also have an impact on *pleasure* as trust and self-esteem can be linked to pleasure. Furthermore the exact way in which a leader is focused on their people will also influence the way in which the basic needs are fulfilled or not. For example, if a people centric leader uses coaching methodology this will indeed have a positive influence on self-esteem and pleasure maximisation. This is however dependent on the individual leader rather than the theory itself.

5.4.3 Situational Theory

Situation theory states that the success of leadership is dependant on given situations and dealing with the situations effectively and successfully. These situations may place very different demands on the leadership and may need different approaches and styles of leadership. The success of leadership will therefore be defined by whether the right style and approach are matched to the specific situation.

Situational leadership was influenced by Fiedler and his Contingency Theory (Fiedler 1967) and Victor Vroom and his research into leadership situations (Vroom and Yetton 1973). The best-known proponents were, however, Paul Hersey and Ken Blanchard (Hersey and Blanchard 1993). In addition to understanding that each situation may need different approaches they defined the situation will be influenced by the leaders' leadership style and the employee's or group's maturity style. The maturity style is defined along two axis one on the level of skills or competence and the other on the level of commitment. From this result four types of maturity:

- **Level 1:** Low competence/high commitment
- **Level 2:** Some competence/low commitment
- **Level 3:** High competence/low commitment
- **Level 4:** High competence/high commitment

The leadership style needs to be adapted to the current situation. Here they defined two dimensions: relationship behaviour and task behaviour (see Sect. 5.4.2).

Relationship styles focus on the relationship with the employees and ensure that they feel good at the workplace and that there is a good relationship to the leader. Task focused approaches place the task in the focus and clear instructions are given combined with guidelines and deadlines to achieve the specific task.

Depending on the maturity level of the employee a different leadership will need to be implemented:

- **Telling:** The employee has little competence but is very interested in and committed to completing the work successfully. This is the employee who is happy to do the work but does not know how. This style gives the clear instructions on how to do the task and how to complete it successfully.
- **Selling:** The employee has some competencies but is not very motivated or committed. Here a leader's role is to give clear instructions on the task and to tap into the individual's emotions to generate motivation. This is also suitable for a coaching style of leadership (see Sect. 5.3.5).
- **Participating:** In this scenario the employee has the suitable competencies but has little motivation or commitment. As the employee has the ability to successfully complete the task the "telling" style is not suitable and the leaders must tap into the emotions and motives of the individual more and be more supportive and participatory.
- **Delegating:** The employee has high competence and is also motivated and committed. For this scenario a delegative approach can be implemented and the employee, as the employee is able to generate their own motivation and has the competencies, can work largely independently.

The maturity model is represented in Fig. 5.16:

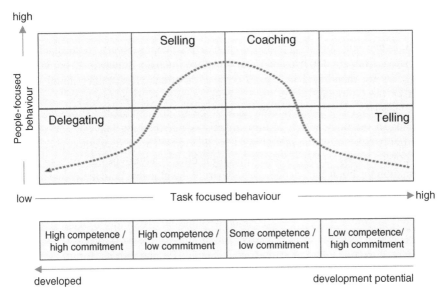

Fig. 5.16 Situational theory (Hersey et al. 2001, p 196)

5.4.3.1 Evaluation

The maturity model for leadership places the employees at the centre of attention and in neuroscientific terms we can see that this understanding enables a satisfaction of the basic needs of the employee. The four levels of maturity allow a situational leadership style that takes into account the employees. The basic need for *orientation and control* is satisfied with the task orientated style whereby the individual is given clear instructions on how to achieve the task. If an individual is unmotivated then their basic need for *pleasure* will need to be stimulated. This focus on the individual also in turn activates the basic need for *attachment* as the focus and relationship is at the forefront of attention.

With employees that have a lack of motivation and commitment then a selling or coaching leadership style should be implemented. This style is targeted more directly at *self-esteem* and its basic need in humans as it is focused on the individual and their relationship with the environment. Through coaching the leaders can tap into the individual talents and underlying drives of the employee. If the individual is competent and highly motivated the leader can then switch to a delegating leadership style that will activate the *orientation and control* basic need as it allows the employees to take control of the situation themselves and also the basic need for *self-esteem* as the respect and authority has been given to the employees showing their value to the team and organisation.

The situational leadership model poses a number of challenges to the leader, as they cannot stick to one style, a natural style maybe, of leadership. A leader will need to assess each situation individually and apply a different style. Also with the understanding that with time the shift, the maturity, should move along the scale to high competence and high motivation, assuming that the leader, or leaders, has managed to tap into the basic needs and skills of each individual.

5.4.4   Emotional Leadership

Emotions can generally be experienced in two dimensions. Firstly on the qualitative dimension, from good to bad and secondly in the intensity dimension from weak to strong. As we mentioned in Sect. 2.6 these emotions affect either mood or are affective, they stimulate action and reactions. As we discussed in Chap. 2 emotions can be described in terms of neurological processes that stimulate various chemical reactions in the body which in turn influences our thinking and our actions and importantly our motivation or abilities to collaborate. This is why emotions are just so important as Watt (1999) noted "Emotions bind together virtually every type of information the brain can encode. . .(it is) part of the glue that hold the whole system together". This is continually underestimated in corporate environments combined with the misunderstanding that emotional leadership means being "emotional" or can get too "touchy, feely". Understanding emotions is simply a healthy human process and is essential to the effective functioning of the workforce.

We touched on Goleman's approach in Sect. 2.7.1 and this is a formulation and process and scheme that leaders can use to approach an emotional style of leadership but also to understand its components (Goleman et al. 2002). We do know that emotions and intellect or higher cognitive functions are at times separate neural circuits but that they also operate in tandem. Yet there is an affect of emotion and emotions can also influence our cognitive functions as we described with fear in Sect. 2.6.2.

A key element of emotional leadership is that of awareness of self and others. This is the prerequisite to understanding one's own emotions but also of being sensitive to and understanding the emotions of others. This also means that the leader must be able to deal with these emotions and to be able to effectively work with them. Building deeper relationships will be a part of this. This ability to understand and respond to emotions will mean that a leader will know, for example, when it is best to just listen or to motivate an employee. This has parallels to situational management which takes the situation as different but uses different descriptive factors and does not box in the styles of emotional representation. Goleman et al. did, however, describe six different types of leadership styles:

- **Visionary leadership:** Visionary leaders develop powerful visions and motivate and encourage and empower their employees to get to this shared vision. This can create a stimulating atmosphere and give rise to strong group coherence, as each person's contribution to the vision is valued.
- **Coaching leadership:** Coaching leaders help their employees by getting to understand their strengths and weaknesses and by hence tapping into these attributes and deeper drives. Coaching leaders show faith, delegate and give responsibility. Their goal is to improve the ability of each employee and understand that these are individuals with different drives and skills and competencies.
- **Affiliative leadership:** The affiliative leader creates harmony within the workplace and connects to the emotions and individuals within their domain. It is a collaborative style of leadership and places emotions over tasks and specific

actions. It aims to tap into the internal emotional drives and hence to build the strong emotional connection which will drive performance.

- **Democratic leadership:** The democratic leader values input and the opinions and idea of the group of employees. They will engage in others' ideas and consider and work through these. Employees will be able to state their opinion and the leader will aim to come to a group consensus that ties in with their goals. Democratic leadership is also a very communicative form of leadership as it involves dialogue in different forms.
- **Pace-setting leader:** The pace-setting leader builds exciting goals and challenges and is exemplary at implementing and showing the pace themselves. They are demanding and expect excellence but through their participatory style can activate emotions and hence create an exciting environment. They will identify the lower performers and expect more of them and will roll up their sleeves and jump in to help drive the situation forward.
- **Commanding leadership:** The commanding leader takes control and gives clear and direct instructions and in this end can give a powerful direction and this strong stance can give a sense of strength and power. He will demand and instruct and actions must be carried out to the word and quickly and efficiently. The commanding leader may seem cold and distant. This style of leadership is best suited to crises and turnaround situations where there is no time for discussion and actions need to be taken quickly and a strong message needs to be given.

5.4.4.1 Evaluation

Goleman's model of emotional leadership is tightly linked to neuroscience and this was the basis for a lot of his propositions: by looking into the way the brain is wired and the connections with the limbic, the emotional systems, and their effect on persons he came to the conclusion that emotional leadership is the only way forward. Indeed any leader per se must be using emotional leadership in some form but especially clearly in areas where no hierarchical constructs demand following. Indeed the definition of a leader as opposed to the definition of a manager requires an element of emotional leadership. A leader must have followers and followers follow emotionally—emotions are therefore simply a necessary part of the equation. This often falls into place without an external cognitive control. Goleman's approach has simply been to try to explain the underlying neuronal processes and the manifestations of successful leadership and in doing this has developed a model that will help more people to be better leaders.

By default we would expect emotional leadership, if it is well formulated, to be able to satisfy all the basic needs. This because if we are taking emotions to represent the whole scale of human interactions and the basic needs as the underlying schemata that require fulfilment, then these should be aligned indeed.

The basic need for *attachment* is approached in many forms whether it be the emotional bonding or need for being listened to. The different styles of leadership that we outlined will have a different impact on this. Emotional leadership is likely to create more powerful bonding through the expression of emotion. Likewise visionary leadership develops a group vision creating unified social goals. Democratic leadership through involving the group has the potential to build strong ties as will a coaching style though this may be limited to the bonding and attachment to the leader themselves.

Various elements of *orientation and control* will be satisfied with the different leadership styles. Visionary styles though giving less immediate direction set a powerful guiding vision and enables employees more control to reach the vision themselves. Coaching styles will allow the understanding for the realisation of more personal control for many as will democratic leadership. Command leadership can give strong direction for some but this style may aggravate those who like to have more autonomy.

Emotional leadership through its focus on emotions is predestined to satisfy the basic need for *pleasure*. This again may depend on the leadership style: coaching and affiliative leadership will be best suited to stimulate more pleasure as these approach the needs and the emotions of each individual. Yet, as we noted in the section on rewards in Sect. 2.4.2, social and respectful environments can lead to reward centre activation and the respect given in democratic styles and the excitement of a visionary leader all have the potential to increase the pleasure experienced in the working place. The commanding style is unlikely to have an impact on pleasure.

Self-esteem a core focus of emotional leadership in general as the value of the emotion and respectively the employee themselves are at the forefront of all the leadership styles. Emotional leadership in general is likely to build most self-esteem and this will be driven by almost all the styles of leadership mentioned above.

5.4.5 Management by Objectives

"Management by" concepts give a set of recommendations for leading. The theory of management by objectives, first popularised by Peter Drucker in his 1954 classic "The Practice of Management" (Drucker 1954), is the principle of developing joint goals and thereby giving clarity to the work process. Management by objectives is based on the following principles.

- **Objective focus rather than process focus:** in place of expecting certain behaviours the leadership will agree on objectives with their employees. The employees can then decide on which behaviours and methods are best to achieve these goals.
- **Regular objective monitoring and adaptation:** the objectives should be continually monitored and adapted where necessary. Because of the ever-changing corporate environment and changing dynamics it will always be necessary to review and modify objectives.
- **Participation of employees in the formation of objectives:** mutual agreement on objectives guarantees that the needs of the employees are taken into account

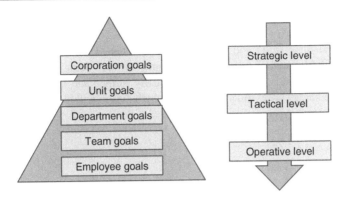

Fig. 5.17 Objective formation

and also their relevant skills, knowledge and specialities. This leads to more realistic objectives and objectives that employees can identify with.

- **Control and appraisal:** leadership and employees need to continually control their objectives. Objectives form the basis of performance reviews and ratings and this will give a shared vision. This will enable a better analysis and continual correction.

This approach will, when applied across an organisation, give rise to an objective hierarchy from broad concrete goals which will then be drilled down to units, departments, teams and individuals (see Fig. 5.17).

5.4.5.1 Evaluation

Management by objectives, if implemented well, has the potential to satisfy practically all the basic needs.

The formulation of objectives in mutual agreement between leadership and employees will lead to more *orientation and control*. The ability to help define the objective enables employees to have some control over their environment. As the goals are clearly defined and aligned with the corporate objectives orientation is clear and fulfilled.

Attachment is not directly influenced by management by objectives. At the same time, if there is respectful communication and discussion and negotiation of objectives, this can in some ways increase the attachment and bonding in an environment but this will be dependant on implementation, people and how intensive and what form the objectives are negotiated.

A key component and background in management by objectives is that the goals are negotiated by employees who know their skills and competencies best. By negotiating goals that tie into these this will not lead to being over challenged on the contrary it can will stimulate the feeling of reward and comfort and maintain a high level of satisfaction with the work. This will directly influence *pleasure* and by negotiating goals that are within one's skill set we have pain avoidance.

Self-esteem in management by objectives is supported in many ways. Firstly through leadership allowing employees to actively take part in the formulation of objectives, the management is showing a deeper level of respect and trust in the employee and groups of employees: this represents a value for the employees their opinions and their skills and competencies and hence the potential to strongly activate the basic need of self-esteem. Secondly through being able to be involved in forming these goals, these can be realistically formed and this will more likely lead to these being successfully completed which in turn will lead to a boost in self-esteem.

5.4.6   Coaching

The prime goal of coaching is to allow the individual to fulfil their potential, to enable them to perform to their best and to unleash their skills and find the blocks that are obstructing this. The coach is often an external coach or an internal coach if the corporation has set up such coaching programmes. It can however, be the leader, and in ideal situations the leader will always be taking on the role to a certain extent. If coaching is about enabling employees to fully realise their potential, and it is, then it must be the role of the leader to stimulate and accompany this process. This in itself brings us to the core definition of a leader vs. a manager in this context a manager will manage performance and control it a leader will enable it to grow and develop into something more powerful.

Coaching by definition is individual as it is dealing with an individual's personal potential and their individual goals. Here we must also distinguish between a trainer and a coach—though many trainers also work as coaches there is a fundamental difference that is important to note. A coach works with an individual and allows the individual to grow—this is driven by the coachee. It is an inside out process. A trainer is the expert and gives or instils the knowledge and tools. It is an outside in process. There is also a fundamental difference between a mentor and a coach. A mentor should have experience and guide and support. A coach taps into the internal processes and power of an individual.

As we are looking at coaching in a leadership context we will look here at how leaders can approach this rather than an external coaching programme. Some corporations have implemented coaching cultures whereby the leaders are trained in coaching processes and the corporation uses a mix of internal coaching, external coaching and coaching processes by the leaders themselves. Depending on the context and needs.

In coaching we can also broadly define two contexts of coaching: firstly developmental when the purpose is to develop an individual and secondly intervention when a high performing individual has suddenly hit problems and a coach is brought in to help the individual redress the situation.

In understanding the role of a leader as a coach we must also understand their way of dealing with people and by definition to take on the role of a coach there must be emotional intelligence and a belief in the person they are dealing with. Coaching, by definition, must take in place in a field of trust and mutual understanding and willingness of the coachee. If this is not met the basis for coaching is not present and a coaching process is likely to be doomed to failure.

There are many models of coaching all designed to tap into the individual. Underlying philosophies may differ and some go into the direction of underlying schemata at a deeper personal and fundamental human level. Some of these are best left to specialist coaches in the field.

In a corporate context Egan's "Skilled Helper" is a simple three-step model that that defines the current state, the preferred state and the actions to get to this preferred state (Egan 1997). With a similar approach the GROW model has been well used and received in corporate contexts (Whitmore 2002):

- Goal setting
- Reality checking
- Options
- What (when, who will)

We can see the similarities between these two models their fundamental base is understanding the current situation and seeing and finding a path forward to a different point. In corporate contexts the leader has many roles but is not a professional coach and the restraints of time and responsibility may hinder a leader, even if willing, to enter into deeper more formal coaching conversations with their employees. Hence we propose an even simpler version of this based on our understanding of basic needs and neural networks. The **UP model:**

- **Understand** what is happening in the current situation. Especially the person, the basic needs and the current environment.
- **Project and plan** the future based on this understanding and the personal needs of the individual.

U and P will operate together and are intrinsically linked and there will need to be a continual back and forth from Understanding to Projection and Planning and actions in a consistent feedback loop. Hendre Coetzee, a leading US-based executive coach, notes the importance of "meaningful conversations". These meaningful conversations will lead to an understanding and a stimulation of action but the goal of coaching is always to move to a newer set of behaviours and it is this that allows a coachee to fulfil their potential.

5.4.6.1 Evaluation

Coaching as a personal strategy based on the individual has the greatest potential to fulfil all basic needs and to fulfil them well.

The need for initial trust is a prerequisite for a coaching process and the closer and more personal interaction with an external coach or the leader-as-coach will provide a strong basis for the building up of a positive relationship founded on deeper understanding of the individual. This is a powerful experience and leads to stronger attachment and bonding. This basis of understanding will stimulate more personal relationships in a positive way and lead to this tighter and closer bonding and therefore fulfil the basic need for *attachment*.

In a coaching context the coachee is the person who defines the goals and direction is only facilitated by the coach or leader as a coach. Therefore in coaching the coachee will always be in control and can be helped to define more specific goals for themselves and this will create and fulfil the basic need for *orientation and control*. The regular meetings and feedback and collaboration will lead to a high level of orientation and understanding of how far the coachee is along the path to achieving their stated goals.

Coaching takes place in a safe context and so pain is avoided because the path for pleasure is opened up. In addition coaching by default looks into increasing the skills and potential of an individual and will inherently be involved with stimulating more pleasure through a deeper understanding of what a coachee needs. Through the release and support of their potential this will lead to more success and less pain fulfilling the basic need for *pleasure maximisation and pain avoidance.*

Being assigned a coach is also a powerful message of respect and value and this already has the potential to boost the self worth and the basic need for *self-esteem* of a coachee. But the coaching process is so designed so as to enable the coachee to develop and build their potential and this will also include potentially building their self–esteem. In defining and forming goals that a coachee can reach and fulfil this will in turn lead to a positive cycle of feeling success and increasing their self worth and value.

Coaching culture models are therefore powerful tools to enhance corporations and when implemented correctly and well have the potential to generate and fulfil all the basic needs and this will lead to healthy and stimulating organisations that are functioning at their optimum.

5.5   Summary

- We can define and evaluate instruments in organisational and personal development in the light of neuroscientific research and processes. We can tie this to the **four basic needs** of humans.
- Depending on what basic need should be developed or approached we can choose to apply various standard **instruments of organisational and personnel development** (Table 5.1):

Table 5.1 Evaluation of selected instruments of organisational and personnel development

	Attachment	Orientation and control	Self-esteem and protection	Pleasure maximisation and pain avoidance
Job enlargement			•	
Job rotation	•		•	•
Jon enrichment		•	•	
Autonomous working groups	•	•		
Job characteristics model	•		•	•
Flow model		•		•

Table 5.2 Evaluation of leadership concepts

	Attachment	Orientation and control	Self-esteem and protection	Pleasure maximisation and pain avoidance
Trait theory	•			
Behavioural theory	•	•		
Situational theory	•	•	•	
Emotional leadership	•	•	•	•
Management by objectives		•	•	•
Coaching	•	•	•	•

- Standard **leadership concepts** can also be seen in the light of neuroscientific research and the four basic needs Table 5.2.

Practical Applications

6

The previous chapters have taken you, the reader, through the journey of the brain, key protagonists, the four basic needs and how these can be influenced by various organisational and personnel development tools. This chapter now aims to take you one step further and into how you can implement this knowledge in a structured way into business contexts. We present the ACTIVE model—a methodology around the four basic needs and this provides a structured approach to applying the knowledge of neuroleadership in the working place. Specifically by being able to analyse the basic needs and their satisfaction in individuals and from this adapt and modify your leadership style and the organisational tools you decide to implement.

Objectives

- Present the ACTIVE model
- Give a practical approach for implementing the knowledge of neuroleadership with relevance to the four basic human needs
- Introduce the PERFECT scheme defining the characteristics of the neuroleader

6.1 Introduction

So far we have taken you on a journey from the concept of man, through understanding the brain. We have looked at other protagonists in the field and we have looked at the four basic needs that are based on neural representations in the brain. We have looked at, in Chap. 5, concrete organisational approaches through the spectacles of neuroscience and the four basic needs. So far we have done most of what we have set out to do. This we defined as giving you a complete overview of neuroleadership. We have taken a good look at the four basic needs and we can now understand organisational tools and leadership concepts through the light of the neuroscientific basic needs. This final chapter we move into a more individualised

A. Ghadiri et al., *Neuroleadership*, Management for Professionals,
DOI 10.1007/978-3-642-30165-0_6, © Springer-Verlag Berlin Heidelberg 2012

and concrete approach. An approach that you can now immediately take away and implement in your workplace. This is a tool that is designed for you to be able to use the knowledge we have presented in this book in an easy to understand format.

We therefore present the ACTIVE model that represents a structured approach to implementing the concepts we have highlighted over the previous pages. This is supported by solid neuroscientific research and brings the concept of neuroleadership into a concrete form in the workplace.

6.2   ACTIVE Model

The ACTIVE model is designed as a tool to enable leaders to form a healthy brain-focused workplace that is solidly founded on neuroscience. This is combined with selected (as outlined in Chap. 5) organisational and personnel development instruments and leadership concepts. The model is designed with the four basic needs as the basis, because these drive and form motivation, and this will therefore enable the fulfilment of these needs to form workplaces where employees can fulfil their true potential for the benefit of the organisation.

These five steps of this approach allow leaders to implement a structured and scientifically solid approach to leadership. The five steps are as follows Fig. 6.1:

- **Analysis:** Analysing and collecting the information which shows the "current" situation and the "preferred" situation with relation to the basic needs of employees.
- **Consistency profile:** creation of a consistency profile for the workplace.
- **Transformation:** placing employees into the two types of "GO-type" and "NO-type" based on their consistency profile and their motivational schemata.
- **Inconsistency avoidance:** choice of instruments from organisational and personnel development and leadership concepts to avoid inconsistency and promote consistency within the four basic needs.
- **VErification:** agreement between employees of the results and the next steps to be taken.

6.2.1   Analysis

The ACTIVE model collects the information that represents the current perceived reality of the workforce and individual employees. This first step is important to be able to gain an insight into each individual employee and how they are interacting with the workplace and how this is personally perceived according to their schemata. Here we will also gain an insight into how they prefer to be lead and under what conditions.

This step of analysis is the basis for all the following steps as it places the consistency of the employee in the focus. As we have discussed this consistency is subjectively experienced state and the individual will be continually looking to move to a level of consistency. This step is to provide an insight into the host of

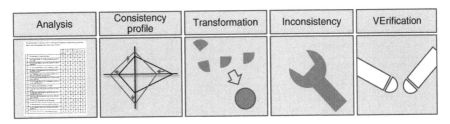

Analysis	Consistency profile	Transformation	Inconsistency	VErification

Fig. 6.1 The five steps of the ACTIVE model

psychological and neuronal processes that form into the experienced representation of the world and the environment an individual is dealing with. This will hence allow us to create and focus on deficiencies and where, for a specific individual, it is possible to improve the experience of the workplace. In bringing the personal level of consistency into balance the leader and corporation will be putting the individual into the potential of having a more satisfying, fulfilling and resonating experience at the workplace and this will drive the human being to higher levels of motivation, more efficient thought processes, better collaboration and less mistakes.[1]

The analysis of consistency can be done in two ways:

- Consistency questionnaire
  -or-
- Consistency interview

We will illustrate and give examples of these two techniques. We include a questionnaire, as an example. We will also give interview guidelines. The first step in this process is to uncover the current state (the "is" state)—the current perceptions and experiences of the working place. The next stage is to glean information of the preferred future situation—the "should" situation. This also highlights which of the basic needs have particularly importance to the individual and how important change is for this particular individual.

The questions relating the "is" and "should" states are based on the four basic needs of *attachment, orientation and control, pleasure* and *self-esteem*. This will be based on work contexts and include elements such as relationship with superiors, personal competencies, satisfaction, etc. to enable us to record various facets of the experience of work and to be able to take into account various facets of the basic needs. We have defined four questions for each basic need for the current scenario and four questions for the preferred scenario. This gives a total of 16 questions for each scenario.

(1) Consistency questionnaire in the workplace

The consistency questionnaire allows middle and larger organisations to gain insights into consistency in an efficient and consistent way that uses far less resources than interviewing. This will need to be clearly explained to employees

---

[1] Chapter 4 discusess the background to this—here we simply present the schematic model as a tool with a structured approach.

		Never	Occa-sionally	Some-times	Gener-ally	Always
1	We work in groups or teams.	☐	☐	☐	☐	☐
2	My colleagues support me and I have a good relationship with my superior.	☐	☐	☐	☐	☐
3	I can talk to my superior when I have problems.	☐	☐	☐	☐	☐
4	I have a good relationship to my superior.	☐	☐	☐	☐	☐
5	We are given responsibility and free room to operate in the work place.	☐	☐	☐	☐	☐
6	My superior keeps me informed on the status of my work and the goals to be achieved.	☐	☐	☐	☐	☐
7	I can influence my working environment to be able to reach my goals.	☐	☐	☐	☐	☐
8	I feel good in the working place and have control over my environment.	☐	☐	☐	☐	☐
9	I feel respected in the company.	☐	☐	☐	☐	☐
10	In my working environment I am respected and appreciated.	☐	☐	☐	☐	☐
11	I have experienced success in my role in the company.	☐	☐	☐	☐	☐
12	My self-esteem is boosted within the company	☐	☐	☐	☐	☐
13	My work is challenging.	☐	☐	☐	☐	☐
14	I enjoy my work.	☐	☐	☐	☐	☐
15	My tasks are varied.	☐	☐	☐	☐	☐
16	I can develop and learn through my work.	☐	☐	☐	☐	☐

Fig. 6.2 Consistency questionnaire, part 1

specifically what the goals are in order to avoid misunderstandings and to ensure that it is answered well. It is also plausible to replace other employee surveys and questionnaires with the consistency questionnaire as this ties into the basic needs and hence the motivational schemata and hence employee satisfaction. An example of a questionnaire is given in Figs. 6.2 and 6.3:

(2) Consistency interview at the workplace

The consistency interview is a qualitative approach to systematically gain information from the employee on their basic needs in the workplace. This is based around an interview, following the guidelines below, that allows the leader to ask specific questions on the employees basic needs and their fulfilment and ideal situations.

The interview should systematically ask questions related to the basic needs and the consistency questionnaire will form the basis of this. It is conceivable that the items can be replaced with other similar and specific questions related to the

		Untrue	Partly true	Gener-ally true	Mostly true	True
1	I enjoy working in groups and teams.	☐	☐	☐	☐	☐
2	I would like to have a closer working relationship with my colleagues and superior.	☐	☐	☐	☐	☐
3	With challenging tasks I look to cooperate with my superior or colleagues	☐	☐	☐	☐	☐
4	It is important for me to have a good relationship to my superior.	☐	☐	☐	☐	☐
5	I enjoy work more when I have more free space and flex-ibility.	☐	☐	☐	☐	☐
6	I work better when I have clear goals and instructions.	☐	☐	☐	☐	☐
7	If I can influence my environment I feel more satisfied.	☐	☐	☐	☐	☐
8	It is important to me to be able to influence my working environment to achieve my goals.	☐	☐	☐	☐	☐
9	I feel better if I am treated respectfully.	☐	☐	☐	☐	☐
10	My positive points are appreciated.	☐	☐	☐	☐	☐
11	The company treats my achievements as importantly as I do personally.	☐	☐	☐	☐	☐
12	If I am happy I have a high level of self-esteem.	☐	☐	☐	☐	☐
13	I enjoy challenges at work.	☐	☐	☐	☐	☐
14	I feel better as a person if I enjoy my work.	☐	☐	☐	☐	☐
15	I am happier if my job has more variety.	☐	☐	☐	☐	☐
16	I want to improve and develop myself through my work.	☐	☐	☐	☐	☐

Fig. 6.3 Consistency questionnaire, part 2

specific context while keeping the background essence similar and particularly the relevance to the basic needs. Keeping the number of questions and the weighting should, however, be kept the same to ensure a correct balance and no distortion in the weighting and resulting profile (see Sect. 6.2.2). An interview holds a number of advantages over the self-reporting method.

- Especially in those cases when a leader is able to engage the employee in an open and authentic conversation the precise question is not necessary which may disturb the flow of conversation and authenticity of the dialogue which in itself will open up the real perspectives of how the employee feels. This will enable a deeper and more authentic view of the basic needs of the individual.
- If the questions are not so clear to the employee, or their interpretation, the leader can immediately react to this and give more context and guide as to how precisely it should be answered.

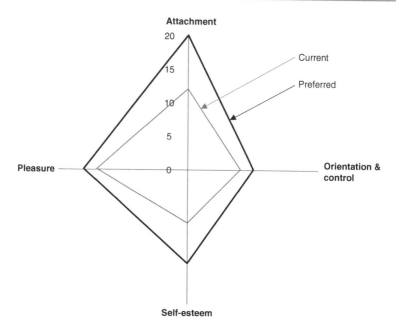

Fig. 6.4 Example of a consistency profile

- An interview is particularly suitable for new employees allowing to get to know this person individually on the basis of their basic needs.

At the same time it is important to highlight that the simple presence of the leader will influence the answers of the employee and will consciously or unconsciously give different answers than in an anonymous situation. An external interviewer would help to solve this problem.

Both approaches have advantages and disadvantages and the specific situation of the organisation and the leader will influence which approach to take.

6.2.2   Consistency Profile

The second step is to analyse the data from the two parts of the consistency questionnaire. The first part gives the results of the current state and the second part gives the results of the preferred state. These results are then transferred to the consistency profile. This gives a diagrammatic representation of the current and preferred state and clearly shows the leaders how closely employees' basic needs are fulfilled in addition to highlighting the personal preferences of basic needs for each individual.

Figure 6.4 shows the consistency profile of a fictional questionnaire. We can see the difference between the current state and the preferred state of the basic needs.

The consistency profile is designed with three single weighted items and one double weighted item (see table 6.1). Single weighted items ask indirect questions

Table 6.1 Scale for the consistency profile

Ranking	Single weighting (Items: 1–3, 5–7, 9–11, 13–15)	Double weighting (Items: 4, 8, 12, 16)
Never/Untrue	0	0
Occasionally/Partly true	1	2
Sometimes/Generally true	2	4
Mostly/Mostly true	3	6
Always/True	4	8

Table 6.2 Valuation of the consistency profile

Block	Item	Sub totals	Total ($\Sigma_{min}/\Sigma_{max}$)
I	1–3	0/1/2/3/4	$\Sigma_{min} = 0 + 0 + 0 + 0 = 0$
	4	0/2/4/6/8	$\Sigma_{max} = 4 + 4 + 4 + 8 = 20$
II	5–7	0/1/2/3/4	$\Sigma_{min} = 0 + 0 + 0 + 0 = 0$
	8	0/2/4/6/8	$\Sigma_{max} = 4 + 4 + 4 + 8 = 20$
III	9–11	0/1/2/3/4	$\Sigma_{min} = 0 + 0 + 0 + 0 = 0$
	12	0/2/4/6/8	$\Sigma_{max} = 4 + 4 + 4 + 8 = 20$
IV	13–15	0/1/2/3/4	$\Sigma_{min} = 0 + 0 + 0 + 0 = 0$
	16	0/2/4/6/8	$\Sigma_{max} = 4 + 4 + 4 + 8 = 20$

on nuances of the relevant basic need. Double weighted items ask direct questions to the basic needs.

The sum will then be calculated for each basic need.

This will then be plotted on a scale of 0–20 (see Table 6.2), on the relevant axis for the basic need. This plotting gives a net diagram and both part 1 and 2 are plotted on this illustrating the differences between the current and preferred scenarios and also the particular importance of each basic need for each individual. This will highlight diagrammatically how important each basic need is for each individual and to what extent this is fulfilled in the workplace. This will also therefore highlight what areas are unfulfilled and where leaders will need to make changes and take action to bring these into balance.

6.2.3 Transformation

The third step is to compare the consistency profile with the behaviours of the employee. For this the behavioural aspects of the individual will need to be analysed. We can do this in three ways:

- **Observation of the leader:** From their experience with their employees an experienced leader will be able to identify those employees with approach or avoidance tendencies (for motivational schemata see Sect. 4.5).
- **Self evaluation of employees:** in a personal talk with an employee they will be able to show how they would rate themselves. The leader can help to give examples and help illustrate what is precisely meant by each category.

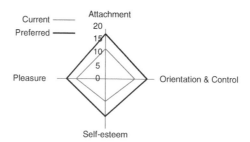

Fig. 6.5 GO-type

- **Through a personality test:** If a behavioural scheme cannot be assessed through the leader or a personal evaluation then we can gain insights into the motivational schemata with a Five Factor test or a questionnaire based on FAMOS (see Sect. 4.5).

After evaluating a tendency for an approach scheme or an avoidance scheme the leader should be able to place the employee into one of two broad categories. These two categories are based on the two consistency theory models (see Sect. 4.3):

- If the employee is approach oriented, they will be active and proactive in fulfilling their basic needs. They will be high in drive and motivation and we call this the **GO-type**. The GO employee will like taking on challenges and can process failures quickly and will generally work well and collaborate well with colleagues.
- The **NO-type** is the employee who has avoidance tendencies. They will be cautious and be more seriously impacted by negative experiences and failures and will tend to protect their basic needs from further damage.

The consistency profile from step 2 illustrates and will clarify the categorisation. The GO-type will actively aim to fulfil their basic needs. Figure 6.5 shows a hypothetical case where an employee has not fulfilled their basic needs. As a GO-type he would, however, like to reach these goals. These also despite high scores on the scales.

The GO-type, we project, will account for the majority of employees and it is reasonable to assume that an employee will actively strive to increase the satisfaction of the basic needs and balance out any deficits and hence will move close to satisfying their basic needs.

Nevertheless we will inevitably also have NO-types that will be inconsistent and their profiles will also be differently represented. Here we give three different types based on forms of consistency profiles (Fig. 6.6):

- **Variation 1:** The individual is avoidant and would like to protect his basic needs in place of trying to extend them. The current and preferred situation are therefore presented as equal—even though the satisfaction of the needs is not actually very high which would normally imply that there would be a drive to satisfy them. This is not the case.

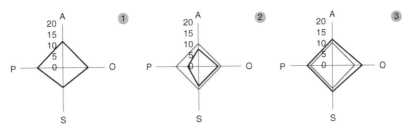

A = Attachment
O = Orientation and Control
S = Self-esteem
P = Pleasure

Fig. 6.6 Three different NO-types

- **Variation 2:** It is also feasible that an avoidant individual will have a preferred rating lower than the current rating. Here we will see a motivational conflict in achieving and fulfilling basic needs. We will potentially see a compensation pattern here meaning another basic need will be driven at the cost of others.
- **Variation 3:** An avoidant individual's preferred state may lie moderately above their current state. However, noticeable is that both are at low levels. This represents an employee who is afraid of change.

In all variations of the NO-type it is particularly important to identify which particular basic need has the strongest avoidance scheme. For example, a person could be attachment avoidant through previous negative experience with their former superior. However, in the context of orientation and control this same person may be approach focused as they work independently and have free space to organise their work. This highlights that the basic needs and their fulfilment can be pursued independently of each other even though they are often interlinked.

6.2.4 Inconsistency Avoidance

The fourth step is the choice of instruments by the leader in order to regulate or specifically target various basic needs and to avoid inconsistency. Here the leader can choose the various organisational and personal developmental and leadership concepts that we presented in Chap. 5. These we have summarised with their suitability to approach various basic needs.

These instruments are particularly suited to GO-types as these will actively pursue the fulfilment of the basic needs and the instruments allow this. In those cases on the consistency profile when the preferred scenario lies above the current scenario.

Please note that our aim in the book has been to analyse a selected number of well-known instruments that we present again in Table 6.3. There are many other ways and interventions and tools to approach this. We hope this book and the discussion of basic needs has shed light on the thinking process and how to analyse a tool or instrument according to their basic needs. Here are some more examples:

Table 6.3 Overview of instruments and models

		Attachment	Orientation & control	Self-esteem	Pleasure
Organisational and personnel development	Job enlargement			•	
	Job rotation	•		•	•
	Job enrichment		•	•	
	Autonomous work groups	•	•		
	Job Characteristics	•		•	•
	Flow Model		•		•
Leadership concepts	Trait theory	•			
	Behavioural theory[a]	•	•		
	Situational theory	•	•	•	
	Emotional leadership	•	•	•	•
	Management by objectives		•	•	•
	Coaching	•	•	•	•

[a]Dependant on leadership style, see Chap. 5.4.2.

- Team work
- Project groups
- International exchange
- Training
- Mentoring
- Delegation
- Reward rituals (e.g. employee of the month)
- Home office
- Job sharing

6.2.5   VErification

The fifth step "verification" aims to verify the steps forward in a personal conversation with the employee and to ensure that this will contribute to the consistency of the employee and that they agree to this.

This personal conversation will enable the leader to verify whether the analysis so far has been accurate and to tie in further processes to the basic needs of the individual employee:

- After the leader has chosen the instruments and models the employee will be invited to the conversation—the explicit goal of which is to improve the working conditions of the employee based on their basic needs.
- The employee should then be informed of the instruments and the next steps that these will foresee. The employee should understand what this means for them

personally and what actions they will, as an individual, be required to make. The specific goals will then also be discussed.

- In the ideal case the employee would be and should be enthusiastic about this.[2] If this does indeed tie in to their basic needs. It is important that each person has communicated their expectations and goals clearly. This should where possible be done in writing.

- After the measurable goals have been formulated then the implementation process can begin. This will involve making all necessary changes to the environment necessary for the concepts to be implemented properly.

There will need to be consistent measurement at regular intervals to measure whether these processes are indeed improving the consistency profile and that the employee is performing to the best of their ability. This can be done as part of a regular review process with the ACTIVE model. The consistency profile of an employee will also change over time with various needs being more or less fulfilled and these could have multiple influences, workplace, co-workers, superiors, economic environment, personal situation and so on. This continual analysis of the consistency over time will ensure that the highest level of consistency possible will be achieved and that each individual employee can individually develop themselves.

6.3   Competencies of the Neuroleader

The ACTIVE model gives the basic frame for operation and the technical background, so to speak, to lead in a broader context using the knowledge of neuroscience as a basis for providing an environment that will be brain friendly and individualised. On top of this organisational approach, the leader themselves will need to behave and act in a way that is brain friendly—in short to become a true neuroleader we not only need to implement the consistency model but understand that a the leader's own way of interacting with the world, with employees and the environment, will have a dramatic impact on how employees perceive their work and how they can also fulfil their basic needs—of the employee and of the leader. Fulfilling the basic needs we can see as the foundation of the house but there needs to be a structure built on top of this and a way of interacting with deeper understanding of people and their brains and how brains react to the environment and between and to individuals. For this we propose this simplified model as a guideline for neuroleadership: **PERFECT**.

- **Potential:** develop and support the potential of each employee
- **Encourage:** encourage employees to take on new challenges and develop themselves
- **Response:** give regular and consistent feedback

---

[2] If this is not the case the talk should be used to identify what is conflicting and how the employee sees the profile or resulting actions. This will enable a rapid identification of whether the leader is on the right track and how to change this.

- **Freedom:** allow as much freedom as possible
- **Emotions:** emotional leadership
- **Communication:** regular communication at the same level
- **Transparency:** be transparent in behaviour and communication

(1) Develop and support the potential of each employee

Developing employees is a central concept in modern leadership and one that many companies at least, academically support. The real importance lies in the ability of this development to impact all the basic needs of the employee positively and lead to a high level of consistency. In particular the development of potential will lead to particular high activation of the basic need for self-esteem but there will also be significant impacts on attachment and pleasure. Put into brain terms it is simply the job of the neuroleader to help develop the brains of their employees to the best of their ability. Healthy brains means good business, efficient business and creative business.

The role of the neuroleader and the challenge at the same time is to ensure the consistent and regular development through training programmes and a direction that the employees can be taken within the company either through different roles or increased responsibility, etc. These tie into many organisational concepts and programmes but the real skill of the neuroleader will be in being able to pull out the best of their employees and so push them to better places. This will require having deeper understanding of their drives and wishes and motivations. We mentioned this in the introduction to Chap. 4 but also in understanding the basic needs through the consistency profile we have, we believe, a powerful tool to help in their development. The neuroleader will be able to operate as a coach where and when necessary and this personal development based on each employee's individual needs will be crucial to the success of this.

(2) Encourage: encourage employees to take on new challenges and to develop themselves

The dynamics in the business world have been changing and the speed ever increasing. Life cycles of products are shorter and new technologies are having productive but also disruptive effects on many aspects of business. Leaders cannot avoid this but will need to proactively engage in this process and the current market and business dynamics. This process we can compare to the brain and its inherent plasticity. The brain can adapt to many situations and is continually learning and making new connections. From an employee's point of view, however, if orientation and control are lost this becomes critical and can have widespread negative impacts. This aspect of change is the damaging one—the unforeseen and unforeseeable, the black hole of uncertainty is what, as we have mentioned, will activate the fear centre in the brain with all its negative consequences. Therefore it is the role of the leader to not only create clarity but also to encourage employees to be able to take on this challenge; to build the inherent flexibility in the system and the flexibility of thought patterns and processes; to find new solutions and keep doing so. This requires courage and encouragement and the support of the leader.

If done well this will then lead to an organisation that can learn and be flexible where the pleasure of creating new ideas and finding new solutions will outweigh the fear of the uncertain. This will help to develop the individual and the team and the corporation. The neuroleader will see this and appreciate its value and will be able to help create this environment through their support and encouragement.

(3) Response: regular and consistent feedback

Consistent and regular feedback is one of the most powerful tools of any leader and especially the neuroleader. This is what will drive continual improvement. The feedback however is a key element to orientation and control with respect to own skills and goals—in Csikszentmihalyi's flow model we noted the importance of feedback. Feedback, that is qualified and supportive, will help to develop the skills of each individual. It will moreover keep the interaction between leader and employees closely aligned and allow a more positive working relationship potentially feeding into the other basic needs of attachment and self-esteem.

(4) Freedom: allow freedom

The neuroleader believes that human beings are and can be responsible, self-sufficient and self-motivating. To enable employees to take responsibility the neuroleader will give clear guidelines while giving enough autonomy for the employee to be able to efficiently complete their tasks. This freedom will release energy as it allows individuals room for control and room for movement which will stimulate various basic needs but also generate more creativity. Particularly the basic need for orientation and control will be best fulfilled with this. This will also increase the efficiency of organisations lowering the need for leaders and managers to be continually checking and controlling and allowing the employees to be a part of the thought process. Employees with avoidance tendencies may, however, be avoidant of more control. It is the role of the neuroleader to be able, based on the individual tendencies, to take this into account and generate strategies for individuals and so know who can take on more freedom and how much this will be.

(5) Emotions: emotional leadership

We discussed emotional leadership in 5.4.4 (and emotional intelligence in 2.6.1) as we have noted in various points the brain is wired emotionally. Emotions are a core component of what it is to be a human being. These are what create drives motivation and influences our hormonal balance and the cognitive balance in our brain. In foremost being an emotional leader means being aware of emotional impact and being able to take these into consideration. To be able to best tap into the emotions of employees we need to be able to understand emotions but moreover to be able to understand employees themselves and their drives and motives. But furthermore emotional leadership is also about one's own emotions—understanding and being aware of how each of us is motivated and drives forward. To be able to tap into one's own emotions and to develop one's own personal drive and personal motivation and this in turn will also engage employees (think mirror neurons 2.5.3). Becoming a true, positive and authentic leader will release energy in employees and motivating and stimulating them simultaneously. This will particularly influence positively the basic needs of pleasure and self-esteem.

(6) Communication: regular communication at the same level

Communication has many functions not least a social function. But more importantly communication creates clarity and understanding and so can help powerfully drive the basic need for orientation and control and hance also avoid

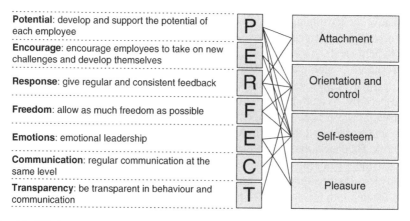

Fig. 6.7 PERFECT scheme

feelings of uncertainty. But the tone and way of communication is also of utmost importance. A basic level of respect needs to be present. This is the basic need for self-esteem. When in hierarchical structures a person speaks down to another we generate layers of people and are implicitly placing people at a lower (or higher level) this will directly impact the feelings of self-esteem. If we treat employees as respected individuals we not only tap into their feeling of self-esteem but allow the freedom for more creative ideas and more positive open and honest dialogue that can also help to avoid negative situations and underlying resentment which remain uncomunicated. We can tie this into Thomas Harris' "I'm ok—you're ok" concept from his best-selling book based on transactional analysis (Harris 1973).

(7) Transparency: in behaviour and communication

A neuroleader will lead with openness and their actions will be clear and open and honest. The employees will need to be able to understand what is happening and see their effect. Words without action will not generate trust and as we noted in Sect. 4.2.1 trust is a basis for business relationships. "Actions speak louder than words" holds true all the time. Transparency also means clarity in communication and personal and corporate goals. When employees know where they are going and how, there is powerful trust in the leadership this provokes a potent cocktail for motivation. It will directly influence the basic need for orientation and control.

To sum up the competencies and skills of a neuroleader Fig. 6.7 shows the PERFECT scheme and its effect on the basic needs.

6.4   Summary

- The ACTIVE model gives leaders a tool to tap into a fundamental level of neuroscientific study which lies at the heart of human nature and behaviours and motivations. The goal of this is to enable systematic use and understanding of various standard organisational and personnel development tools to influence the consistency of employees (and thus tap into their motivational drives). This is spilt into five steps

- **Analyse:** the current state of satisfaction of the basic needs is balanced against the preferred state. This is done through the consistency questionnaire or the consistency interview.
- **Consistency profile:** The results of the analysis are plotted onto a diagram.
- **Transformation:** This step takes the consistency profile and transforms this into the different GO-types or NO-types.
- **Inconsistency:** Here the various instruments and concepts of organisational and behavioural development are chosen and matched to the individual and presented to the employee.
- **VErification:** The last step involves an agreement between the leader and the employee on the changes and the jointly defined goals.
- The competencies and skills that a neuroleader should have to be able to tap into the brain and the basic needs of humans can be summarised in the **PERFECT** scheme:
  - **Potential:** develop and support the potential for each employee
  - **Encourage:** encourage employees to take on new challenges and develop new thinking patterns
  - **Response:** regular and consistent feedback
  - **Freedom:** allow freedom
  - **Emotions:** emotional leadership
  - **Communication:** regular communication at the same level
  - **Transparency:** in behaviour and communication

6.5   Closing Words

You have now come to the end of this journey through the brain, what it is, how it is formed and the biological basis for human interactions. This journey is designed to raise your awareness of what may seem obvious but is not to many—that the brain is at the root of all human interactions and understanding this will help our understanding of systems where human beings are involved. This is the essence of business—all businesses pay tribute to the human capital that they have, but almost all fail in using this to its full potential. Becoming a neuroleader does not mean becoming a neuroscientist but rather developing an understanding of the fundamental functions of the brain and to tie this in to the interactions in the workplace.

The work of Klaus Grawe we have found to be particularly relevant, nay a brilliant and insightful approach at the core of human nature, because this ties in the heart of human nature to the neuronal processes and hence connects directly neuroscience to the brain and to psychology. These basic needs that Grawe defines are at the deeper level of all our human interactions and this is why we have focused on these. This is the foundation on which we aim to build the house of neuro-leadership and indeed on which it *must* be built: without this foundation it will surely crumble. From this there are many specifics, many individual situations where we can look at different neuronal processes. These may be in generating more creativity, in avoiding fear in crises situations, selling to difficult clients, building teams, managing talent, learning processes and in change management. These are important to businesses and leaders also but we are proposing with this book that we go to the base first and from there we can move outward into the specifics of corporate contexts.

The ACTIVE model is tool that you can implement easily and effectively to be able to create clarity around the basic needs in your workforce and to develop targeted interventions and strategies to activate the basic needs of your employees. We have only chosen a number of selected instruments and tools to analyse but hope you will be able to use the knowledge in this book to apply the methodology to other tools also. This is also one of our primary goals—for if you can take the methodology, the understanding of basic needs and motivational schemata we believe this will increase your understanding of the world of human interactions and be a powerful tool in any context that involves human interaction.

We are convinced that if you can understand the basic needs and think through your corporate processes from this point, combined with the wealth of information about the brain, you can truly become a neuroleader. We firmly believe that this will make your life easier, more rewarding and translate into better performance and higher returns in your business. And we are sure this will also be an enjoyable experience. And reward centre activation is key as we have learnt in this book!

Learning Check

7

This is for those who wish to ensure they have taken as much away as possible form this book.

Chapter 1

1. What is the difference between neuroeconomics and neuro business administration?
2. Which neuro business administration disciplines do you know and can you list them?
3. What do you understand with neuroleadership? Give at least two defining factors.
4. How would you describe homo economicus?
5. How did homo sociologicus develop and how is it characterised?
6. How did the concept of complex man differ to the previous concepts?
7. How can we define brain-directed man?
8. What is the relevance of brain-directed man for the workplace and working processes?

Chapter 2

1. What do you understand under "neuroscience"?
2. What is the three-layer model of the brain and what are the specific functions for the regions?
3. What is the process scheme in the brain?
4. Explain what neuroplasticity is and the impact of this on learning.
5. What is the reward system? Can this be stimulated with financial incentives? Why? or Why not?
6. How can the knowledge of mirror neurons help us in daily life?
7. Classify the brain research technologies – which are particularly suitable for research and why?
8. Explain the terms "feeling" and "emotion".

A. Ghadiri et al., *Neuroleadership*, Management for Professionals,
DOI 10.1007/978-3-642-30165-0_7, © Springer-Verlag Berlin Heidelberg 2012

9. What dimensions for emotional intelligence does Goleman define?
10. Name four neuro transmitters and their effects.
11. What are the effects of dopamine and what is its relationship to the reward system?
12. Define "cognitive enhancement".
13. Name two substances or medications that can be used to manipulate performance in the workplace.
14. Describe the stress (HTPA) axis.
15. How can a brain-friendly environment be formed?

Chapter 3

1. Name the five neuroscience-based approaches.
2. Describe the brain dominance concept and the four types.
3. Describe supportive leadership from Hüther and what are the basic rules?
4. What advantages do group conferences have according to brain science?
5. What should leaders do, according to Hüther, when employees make mistakes?
6. What happens, from the brain's perspective when a leader praises an employee for good work?
7. Name the four brain systems that Elger names.
8. What role does the reward system play in Elger's Neuroleadership?
9. What is the relevance of fairness and feedback according to Elger?
10. What is Rock's SCARF model?
11. What are the similarities between Rock's SCARF model and Elger's neuroleadership model?
12. What are the similarities between Rock's SCARF model and Hüther's principles?
13. What is neurocoaching?
14. Where does there need to be more research according to the discussion?
15. Name the current trends in neurocoaching.

Chapter 4

1. What is the purpose of the consistency theory model?
2. What are the four basic needs of the consistency theory model?
3. Describe the functioning of oxytocin with its related basic need. Give an example of this function in the corporate context.
4. What is meant by the basic need for orientation and control? How can a leader take this into account?
5. What differentiates the basic need for self-esteem from the other basic needs?
6. How can a leader positively influence the basic need for pleasure? Tie this to neuronal processes and the brain-processing model.
7. What are the defining characteristics of human behaviour? What are motivational schemata and motivational goals?
8. What are motivational schemata and motivational goals?

9. Explain the difference between approach and avoidance motivational schemata and give an example from daily business.
10. Name and describe how extreme types form the combination of personality psychology and motivational schemata. Support your comments with an example.
11. What do we understand with the term consistency? Give an example of this.
12. How do we achieve congruence? Show this in a diagram and explain the different components.
13. What is incongruence? What types of incongruence are there?

Chapter 5

1. How can organisational and personnel development approaches be aligned with neuroscientific principles? How is this aligned with the four basic needs?
2. How can the basic need of attachment be fulfilled in the workplace? Give an example of this.
3. Why and how can the basic need for orientation and control be best influenced by the leader.
4. How can the basic need for self-esteem be damaged in the work place?
5. What is the relationship between dopamine and the basic need for pleasure?
6. Describe the instruments of job enlargement, job enrichment and job rotation and explain what basic needs can be positively influenced by each.
7. Which basic needs can especially be positively influenced in Autonomous Working Groups?
8. Describe the Job Characteristics Model and which basic needs this can positively influence.
9. What do you understand with "flow"? How is this related to the reward system?
10. Present the trait, behavioural and situational theories and which basic needs are positively influenced by each.
11. What is emotional leadership (according to Goleman)? What six styles of leadership did he identify and how is emotional intelligence linked to this?
12. Which basic needs are stimulated through management by objectives?
13. Why is oxytocin important in coaching contexts?

Chapter 6

1. Describe the ACTIVE model and what are the six steps?
2. What is the purpose of the consistency profile?
3. Describe the GO-type and the NO-type in relationship to the ACTIVE model. What are the different types? Draw these.
4. What is the purpose of the step inconsistency avoidance?
5. What needs to be planned in the step of VErification?
6. Name and explain the competencies of the neuroleader and what relationship these have to the basic needs.

Glossary

Adrenaline Hormone that is released in stress situations and leads to increased blood pressure, heart rate and release of energy reserves.

Affect A passively experienced sensation that represents an emotional stimulus. An affect has a clear trigger.

ACTIVE model Model for practical application of neuroleadership based on neuroscience.

Altruistic punishment The punishment of individuals (or groups) that go against social norms. Altruistic punishment does not seek to gain material benefits but rather to punish unjust behaviours.

Amygdala the amygdalae are subdivided into various nuclei and are widely connected to the other brain regions. They operate as emotional centres and are particularly known for their role in fear and stress reactions but have multiple functions including memory consolidation, optimism and social functioning.

Approach incongruence The intention of individuals to achieve their goals is blocked by avoidance tendencies. Therefore goals are ignored or not followed.

Approach schema The behaviour of an individual that actively follows the satisfaction and fulfilment of their basic needs.

Attachment need The need of an individual for attachment and bonding to an attachment figure. In childhood this will normally be the primary caregiver. In adulthood it will be replaced by bonds and attachments formed to other persons.

Autonomous working groups Task and job enrichment at the level of the group where groups of individuals are given wide-reaching responsibilities and can operate in relative autonomy.

Avoidance schema An individual behaves in such a way as to not actively pursue satisfaction of their basic needs but rather to protect them.

Avoidance incongruence When the drive of individuals to protect their basic needs is overridden with another approach drive. If the goal is not achieved then the basic needs are not protected and this will have widespread negative impact.

Axon Primary transmission line from the cell body in a neuron connecting to other dendrites.

Basal ganglia A group of structures sitting within the limbic system that have numerous functions and consolidatory functions such as motor control, procedural learning, cognitive emotional processing.

A. Ghadiri et al., *Neuroleadership*, Management for Professionals,
DOI 10.1007/978-3-642-30165-0, © Springer-Verlag Berlin Heidelberg 2012

Basic needs The four basic needs according to Grawe that all humans need to satisfy and balance. See also Attachment, Pleasure, Orientation and Control, Self-Esteem.

Behavioural theory Theory that states that leadership success is dependant on the behaviours of the leader.

Belonging Identification of an individual with a group or a person with a unified and overlapping set of beliefs and ideas and goals.

Brain-directed man The concept of man that sees the brain as the basis for actions and reactions and defines the brain's interactions with the environment as the basis for all behaviour.

Brain dominance concept Concept developed by Ned Herrmann that say that different people have different dominances in their use of the brain and this will influence how they process information and interact with the world.

Brain stem Evolutionary seen, the oldest part of the brain sitting at the top of the spinal cord and responsible for homeostasis and primitive reactions and impulses.

Charisma (Trait Theory) An important trait of leaders that has a strong correlation to leadership effectiveness. Charismatic leaders have the ability to engage their employees and impart a strong sense of vision and encourage and motivate people to work towards unified goals.

Cell body The processing centre for nerve cells (neurons) where the entire chemical processing of the cells resides.

Cerebral cortex The outer layer of the brain that has a wide set of functions from sensory input, associations, language, movement, and higher executive functions.

Coaching Development of individuals through personalised interventions based on their own skills abilities and their own ability to grow within themselves.

Cognitive enhancement The targeted use of chemical substances to increase cognitive performance such as concentration, memory, alertness.

Cognitive neuroscience Deals with the activity of the nervous system and the mutual affect on cognitive processes such as decision making, planning and memory.

Confidence (Trait Theory) Leaders with confidence often have this based on numerous previous positive experiences. They are therefore seen by employees as confident and this develops trust in their position and authority. Confidence also generates a strong direction and belief in their actions and decisions.

Congruence If an individual can satisfy their basic emotional needs and acknowledge this we speak of congruence. Congruence is therefore the connection between our experience of the world and our needs and our motivational goals.

Consistency Consistency is the state in which neuronal and psychological processes are in harmony.

Consistency questionnaire Questionnaire to assess the subjective experience of the four basic needs (current and preferred states).

Consistency theory model This model combines the four basic needs and the resulting motivational schemata into a coherent theory.

Control need Basic need that represents the ability to be able to personally control a given situation. This can be promoted through giving individuals as much free room as possible and avoiding an external interference. The control need is tightly linked to the ability to be able to predict the future and have the cognitive knowledge of the situation and how to master it.

Command leadership Style of leadership that is exercised with strict commands and autocratically formed goals.

Cortex See cerebral cortex. Also brain regions (e.g. Occipital Cortex).

Cortisol Hormone that is released in stress situations and that influence a wide range of chemical reactions in the body.

Dendrite Branch of a neuron that receives signals and connects these to the cell body. Neurons can have, depending on the type, thousands of these connections.

Discordance Balance of approach and avoidance tendencies that lead to a mutual blocking and an inability to achieve one's goals and dissatisfaction with the current situation.

Dopamine Hormone that generates feelings of happiness and elation but also influences attentional control and motivation. It is activated through the Ventral Tegmental Area and closely interrelated to the reward system.

Electroencephalogram Technique measuring electrical activity in the brain with electrodes placed on the scalp.

Trait theory States that leadership success is based on the traits – the personality and characteristics of the leader – and defines what the characteristics for success are.

Empathy The ability to put yourself in another person's position and relate to their emotions and feelings.

Emotional leadership The skill of leading through emotional intelligence. In a formalised sense a model of leadership combined with a series of different leadership styles.

Emotional intelligence A set of personal and social competencies that places other's and one's own personal emotions, in the focal point. Leaders with emotional intelligence show an ability to understand and control their own emotions and to be able to identify with other's emotion and to be able to tap into these to generate motivation and harmony. Defined by Goleman in five dimensions: self-awareness, self-regulation, self-motivation, social awareness, social competence.

Extraversion Describing the characteristics of an individual that is focused on the external world and interacts with other individuals. They tend to be open, communicative and enjoy contact with others. Also one of the five factors in the "Big Five" or "Five Factor Model".

Flow The state of optimal experience that manifests as a high motivational state where one may feel separated from the outside world. This was first proposed by Csikzentmihalyi and there are a number of criteria that need to be met for this to take place: clear goals, regular and consistent feedback, balance of challenge to skills, lack of fear and stress.

Functional magnetic resonance imaging (fMRI) Technique for picturing brain activation through measuring the haemoglobin supply in the brain's regions and placing this onto 2-D or 3-D representations.

Five factor model Standard widely accepted personality psychology model that measures five dimensions of personality: neuroticism, extraversion, openness, conscientiousness and agreeableness.

Glucose Simple sugar and primary source of energy for cells.

Hippocampus The hippocampus is generally seen as the memory centre of the brain and sits in the limbic system. Although some forms of memory (spatial, for example) do seem to reside in the hippocampus itself its function is normally that of a memory consolidation centre, helping form these memories which are saved as traces in the whole brain.

Hypothalamus Key part of the limbic system that modulates the pituitary gland.

Incongruence The opposite of congruence in the Consistency Theory Model.

Inconsistency The opposite of consistency in the Consistency Theory Model (see Consistency)

Integrity (Trait Theory) Integrity is defined in trait theory in the context of the leadership relationship with employees and states that the leader will be reliable and honest to their employees.

Intelligence (Trait Theory) defines verbal ability, decision making ability and arguing faculties that give rise to a clear mind and focused attention and problem solving ability. This is related to but not exclusively to the actual IQ score.

Introversion Personality trait that represents a person who is internally focused and will not seek or even avoid the company of others. These individuals tend to be quieter and more reflective in nature. This is the opposite of extraversion and hence also a part of the Five Factor Model.

Job enlargement Increasing the scope of the job with additional related and suitable tasks.

Job enrichment Increasing the scope of the job with increased responsibility.

Job rotation Changing places with another employee in the same organisation, normally at a similar functional level.

Job characteristics model Job definition model that looks into the job and its tasks defines characteristics: skills variety, task identity, task significance, task autonomy, task feedback.

Limbic system The "second" layer of the brain in the three-layer model. The area sitting over the brain stem and under the cerebral cortex where our emotional centres sit.

Magnetoencephalogram Technique measuring electrical currents in the brain through magnetic fields.

Magnetic resonance imaging (MRI) Imaging technique allowing pictorial representation of internal organs.

Management by objectives Leadership technique through defining clear objectives and ensuring the following are met: objective focus, objective monitoring, participation of employees and control and feedback.

Maturity Part of the situational leadership model (see Situational Leadership) which states that employees will have different maturities and hence will need to be led differently. These maturities are defined along the axis of skills and commitment.

Moods are representations of broad emotions in a form that influences an individual over time and colours the way we see the world.

Motivational schemata Set of instruments and drives that an individual has developed over time and their life to satisfy and fulfil their basic needs or in order to protect them.

Motivational goals From the basic needs and the motivational schema come so-called motivational goals. These are formed from the basic needs and the neuronal basis of the brain and the actions that can thus be taken.

Motivational conflict See discordance.

Nervous system The collection of nerve cells and their collection in the complete organism.

Nerve cell See neuron.

Neuro business administration Classification of the disciplines of business administration into the neuroceconomic term. Using the insights of he neurosciences to understand and influence the concepts and functions of business administration.

Neurobiology Neuroscientific discipline dealing with the structure and development of the nerves cells and the various systems.

Neurochemistry The discipline of the chemical processes in the nervous system and particularly the brain.

Neurocoaching Using the knowledge of neuroscience in coaching contexts targeting the brain of the individual.

Neuroleadership Leadership through using the knowledge of the brain and specifically the neuroscientifically founded four basic needs.

Neurology Field of medicine dealing with the diagnosis and therapy of disorders in the nervous system.

Neuron Brain cells that form the base of the brains' communication process. They consist of a cell body, dendrites and an axon.

Neurophysiology Neurophysiology is a sub-discipline of physiology and is the study of the performance and reaction of our nervous system to external stimuli. The focus is on the dynamic processes between nerve cells and how these process information.

Neuropsychology Neuropsychology is the study at the interface of psychology and the neuronal processes that underlie psychological processes in the brain.

Neuropsychotherapy Using neuroscientifically based techniques in the treatment of mental disorders.

Neuroticism Is the trait that lacks emotional stability and neurotic people will be easily emotionally swayed and often express a nervous disposition.

Neurotransmitter An organic chemical substance that is involved in the communication process between synapses of neurons.

Neurosciences Collection of disciplines that look into the breadth of neuronal processes in the brain.

Occipital cortex Region of the brain (at the rear) that is mainly responsible for the visual functions.

Organisational development The analysis and development of the organisation and its employees to increase efficiency and effectiveness of the workforce.

Organisational psychology Science focusing on the experience and perceptions of employees in the workplace in corporate organisational structures.

Orientation need Need to have an overview and to be able to understand a given situation.

Oxytocin Hormone that strongly influences our feelings of trust and bonding. Also helps form closer relationships and loving partnerships.

Participative leadership style Leadership style that involves employees and groups into the decision making process.

Pain avoidance Basic need of humans to avoid unpleasurable, uncomfortable and painful experiences.

People oriented leadership Leadership style that focuses more on the people involved in the process (in contrast to task-focused style).

Personnel development The measures, actions and interventions designed to increase the quality of the workforce along various dimensions: skills, competencies, and roles.

Personality psychology Discipline of psychology that looks into the different characteristic and traits of humans and their empirical research and explanation.

Pituitary gland Gland that controls the hormonal secretion and balance in human beings.

Pleasure Need and drive to experience positive and pleasurable experiences.

Plasticity (of the brain) Ability of the brain to keep building connections for most of human life.

Positron emissions tomography Imaging technique that measures blood supply with mildly radioactive substances in the brain.

Process schema The representation of the decision-making process in the brain.

Psychology Science dealing with mental processes and behaviour.

Reward maximisation Representation of the human desire to increase the amount of pleasurable experiences in contrast to negative.

Reward system A collection of mechanisms in the brain that is responsible for the feelings of reward and happiness, normally associated with the dopamine circuit that stimulates feeling of happiness and elation.

SCARF model David Rock's SCARF model is designed to increase awareness of leaders to different facets of leadership and particular in the social contexts of organisations. These are based on neuronal processes. SCARF stands for: Status, Certainty, Autonomy, Relatedness, Fairness.

Self-awareness (Emotional Intelligence) The ability to be able to introspect and to be aware of one's own feelings and motives and also the effect on others.

Self-motivation (Emotional Intelligence) Ability to work on problems and projects without an external extrinsic reward such as money or status.

Self-regulation (Emotional Intelligence) The ability to control one's impulses and moods. To have your own mood which is not affected by external inputs.

Self-esteem The emotional dimension of personal awareness and the subjective feeling of feeling valued and having a self-worth.

Situational theory Definition of leadership success through the various situations that the workplace presents which will need to be deal with in different ways. Each situation may therefore require different competencies and skills.

Social neuroscience A term from David Rock that emphasises the neuroscientific basis of social interactions.

Social awareness (Emotional Intelligence) See empathy.

Social competence (Emotional Intelligence) Is the ability to adapt to social situations and configurations and in these varying contexts to be able to inspire and influence through effective communication skills and the ability to tap into others' emotions and motives.

Stress Physical and mental strain exerted through external and also subjective stimuli.

Supportive leadership Leadership style that supports, develops and motivates employees.

Synapse Connecting point between a dendrite and an axon. The dendrite and axon do not touch but communicate by releasing chemicals that move across the synaptic gap.

Task analysis Systematic analysis of a task breaking it down into its constituent components.

Task oriented leadership Leadership style whereby the leader focuses on the task, its completion and its goals.

Thalamus The thalamus operates as kind of relay station taking incoming signals and sending them to various parts of the brain for processing. It is sometimes classed in the brain stem and sometimes in the limbic system. It functions as the first entry and sorting point for signals coming into the brain.

Three-Layer model Simplified model of the brain representing it in three layers.

Trust A base human instinct that places people in a positive light that gives security and stability to rely on a person's ability in certain contexts. A core element in bonding and relationship building.

Verification Joint agreement between leader and employee with respect to organisational and operational goals and actions drawn from the consistency profile.

Neuronal connection patterns Formation and connection of neurons together and the pathways and connections that neurons form between each other.

Visionary leadership style Style of leadership that focuses on and develops powerful visions. The leader is also strong in motivating, encouraging and empowering employees to achieve a shared vision.

Bibliography

Adolphs, R. (2003). Cognitive neuroscience of human social behaviour. *Nature Reviews Neuro-science, 4*(3), 165–178.

Allport, G. (1961). *Pattern and growth in personality*. New York: Holt, Rinehart and Winston.

Allen Brain Atlas. *Allen institute for brain science*. Accessed September 16, 2012, from http://www.brain-map.org.

Amir-Zilberstein, L., et al. (2012). Homeodomain protein Otp and activity-dependent splicing modulate neuronal adaptation to stress. *Neuron, 73*(2), 279–291.

Arias-Carrión, O., Stamelou, M., Murillo-Rodríguez, E., Menéndez-González, M., & Pöppel, E. (2010). Dopaminergic reward system: A short integrative review. *International archives of medicine, 3*(1), 24.

Auf dem Hövel, J. (2008). *Pillen für den besseren Menschen. Wie Psychopharmaka, Drogen und Biotechnologie den Menschen der Zukunft formen*. Hannover: Heise.

Backhouse, R. E., & Medema, S. G. (2009). Defining economics: The long road to acceptance of the Robbins definition. *Economica, 76*, 805–820.

Barclay, P. (2006). Reputational benefits for altruistic punishment. *Evolution and Human Behavior, 27*(5), 325–344.

Barrick, M. R., & Mount, M. K. (1991). The big five personality dimensions and job performance: A meta-analysis. *Personnel Psychology, 44*(1), 1–26.

Banks, S. J. et al. (2007). Amygdala – frontal connectivity during emotion regulation. *Comparative and General Pharmacology*, 303–312.

Baumgartner, T., Heinrichs, M., Vonlanthen, A., Fischbacher, U., & Fehr, E. (2008). Oxytocin shapes the neural circuitry of trust and trust adaptation in humans. *Neuron, 58*(4), 639–650.

Bechara, A., Damasio, H., & Damasio, A. R. (2003). Role of the amygdala in decision-making. *Annals of the New York Academy of Sciences, 985*(1), 356–369.

Belbin, R. M. (1981). Management teams: Why they succeed or fail Author: R. Meredith Belbin. *R&D Management, 12*(3), 147–148.

Bigelow, H. J., & Barnard, J. (2002). Phineas gage. *Brain, 3*(2), 843–857.

Blake, R., & Mouton, J. (1964). *The managerial grid: The key to leadership excellence*. Houston: Gulf Publishing Company.

Blinkhorn, S. F. (1997). Past imperfect, future conditional: Fifty years of test theory. *The British Journal of Mathematical and Statistical Psychology, 50*(2), 175–185.

Blue Brain Project. (2012). http://bluebrain.epfl.ch/. Accessed 1 Nov 2012.

Boudreau, C., McCubbins, M. D., & Coulson, S. (2009). Knowing when to trust others: An ERP study of decision making after receiving information from unknown people. *Social Cognitive and Affective Neuroscience, 4*(1), 23–34.

Bowlby, J. (1951). *Maternal care and mental health* (p. 179). Geneva: World Health Organization.

Bowlby, J., Ainsworth, M., & Bretherton, I. (1992). The origins of attachment theory. *Developmental Psychology, 5*, 759–775.

Bracha, H. S., Ralston, T. C., Matsukawa, J. M., Williams, A. E., & Bracha, A. S. (2004). Does 'fight or flight' need updating? *Psychosomatics, 45*(5), 448–449.

A. Ghadiri et al., *Neuroleadership*, Management for Professionals,
DOI 10.1007/978-3-642-30165-0, © Springer-Verlag Berlin Heidelberg 2012

Bracha, H. S., et al. (2004). Does "fight or flight" need updating? *Psychosomatics, 45*(5), 448–449.

Brodmann, K. (1909). *Vergleichende Lokalisationslehre der Grosshirnrinde in ihren Prinzipien dargestellt auf Grund des Zellenbaues*. Leipzig: Verlag von Johann Ambrosius Barth.

Brooks, C. M. (1988). The history of thought concerning the hypothalamus and its functions. *Brain Research Bulletin, 20*(6), 657–667.

Bruce, K. (2006). Henry S. Dennison, Elton Mayo, and Human Relations historiography. *Management and Organizational History, 1*(2), 177–199.

Bruce, L. L., & Braford, M. R. (2009). Evolution of the limbic system. *Encyclopedia of Neuroscience*, 43–55.

Burnham, T., McCabe, K., & Smith, V. L. (2000). Friend-or-foe intentionality priming in an extensive form trust game. *Journal of Economic Behavior & Organization, 43*(1), 57–73.

Camerer, C. F., Loewenstein, G., & Prelec, D. (2004). Neuroeconomics: Why economics needs brains. *Scandinavian Journal of Economics, 106*(3), 555–579.

Camerer, C., Loewenstein, G., & Prelec, D. (2005). Neuroeconomics: How neuroscience can inform economics. *Journal of Economic Literature, 43*(1), 9–64.

Carey, J. (2006). *Brain facts: A primer on the brain and nervous system* (p. 11). Washington, DC: Society for euroscience Society for euroscience.

Carmichael, M. S., Humbert, R., Dixen, J., Palmisano, G., Greenleaf, W., & Davidson, J. M. (1987). Plasma oxytocin increases in the human sexual response. *The Journal of Clinical Endocrinology and Metabolism, 64*(1), 27–31.

Casse, R., Rowe, C. C., Newton, M., Berlangieri, S. U., & Scott, A. M. (2002). Positron emission tomography and epilepsy. *Molecular Imaging and Biology, 4*(5), 338–351.

Cast, A. D., & Burke, P. (2002). A theory of self-esteem. *Social Forces, 80*(3), 1041–1068.

Coffield, F., Moseley, D., Hall, E., Ecclestone, K., & Corporate Author Learning and Skills Research Centre (U.K.) (LSRC). (2004). *Learning styles and pedagogy in post 16 learning a systematic and critical review*. London: Learning and Skills Research Centre.

Corbetta, M., & Shulman, G. L. (2002). Control of goal-directed and stimulus-driven attention in the brain. *Nature Reviews Neuroscience, 3*(3), 201–215.

Costa, P. T., & McCrae, R. R. (1992). *Professional manual: Revised NEO personality inventory (NEO-PI-R) and NEO five-factor inventory (NEO-FFI)*. Odessa: Psychological Assessment Resources.

Cowen, W. M., & Kandel, E. R. (2001). A brief history of synapses and synaptic transmission. In W. M. Cowen, T. C. Südhof, & C. Stevens (Eds.), *Synapses* (pp. 1–88). Baltimore: John Hopkins University Press.

Csikszentmihalyi, M. (1991). *Flow: The psychology of optimal experience* (1st ed.). New York: Harper Perennial.

Cunningham, J. B., & Eberle, T. (1990). A guide to job enrichment and design. *Personnel, 67*(2), 56–61.

Davis, M. (1997). Neurobiology of fear responses: The role of the amygdala. *The Journal of Neuropsychiatry and Clinical Neurosciences, 9*(3), 382–402.

Davis, M., & Whalen, P. J. (2001). The amygdala: Vigilance and emotion. *Molecular Psychiatry, 6*(1), 13–34. Available at: http://www.ncbi.nlm.nih.gov/pubmed/11244481.

Davidson, R. J., Jackson, D. C., & Larson, C. L. (2000). Human electroencephalography. In J. T. Cacioppo, L. G. Tassinary, & G. G. Berntson (Eds.), *Handbook of psychophysiology* (Vol. 2, pp. 27–52). New York: Cambridge University Press.

Devauges, V., & Sara, S. J. (1990). Activation of the noradrenergic system facilitates an attentional shift in the rat. *Behavioural Brain Research, 39*(1), 19–28.

Digman, J. M. (1990). Personality structure: Emergence of the five-factor model. *Annual Review of Psychology, 41*(1), 417–440.

Dolan, R. J. (2007). The human amygdala and orbital prefrontal cortex in behavioural regulation. *Philosophical Transactions of the Royal Society of London. Series B, Biological Sciences, 362* (1481), 787–799.

Drucker, P. F. (1954). *The practice of management*. New York: Butterworth-Heinemann.

Duman, E. A., & Canli, T. (2010). *Serotonin and behavior* (Vol. 21, pp. 449–456). Elsevier B.V.

Dumas, G., Nadel, J., Soussignan, R., Martinerie, J., & Garnero, L. (2010). Inter-brain synchonization during social interaction. *PLoS One, 5*(8), e12166.

Egan, G. (1997). *Skilled helper: A problem-management approach to helping* (6th ed.). Belmont: Wadsworth.

Eisenberger, N. I., Inagaki, T. K., Muscatell, K. A., Byrne Haltom, K. E., & Leary, M. R. (2011). The neural sociometer: Brain mechanisms underlying state self-esteem. *Journal of Cognitive Neuroscience, 23*(11), 3448–3455.

Ekman, P., Friesen, W. V., & Ellsworth, P. (1982). *Emotion in the human face* (Vol. 2, p. 464). Cambridge: Cambridge University Press.

Elger, C. E. (2009). *Neuroleadership*. Planegg /München: Haufe.

Epstein, S., & Weiner, I. B. (2003). Cognitive-experiential self-theory of personality. In M. J. Lerner (Ed.), *Comprehensive handbook of psychology volume 5 personality and social psychology* (Vol. 5, pp. 159–184). Hoboken: Wiley.

Eysenck, H. J. (1967). The biological basis of personality. Springfield: Charles C Thomas.

Eysenck, H. J., & Eysenck, M. W. (1985). *Personality and individual differences: A natural science approach*. New York: Plenum Press.

Feinstein, J. S., Adolphs, R., Damasio, A., & Tranel, D. (2010). The human amygdala and the induction and experience of fear. *Current Biology, 21*(1), 1–5.

Feist, E., & Primis, H. (2010). *Psychology: Making connections*. Boston: McGraw-Hill.

Fiedler, F. F. (1967). *A theory of leadership effectiveness* (Vol. 111, no. 2, p. 310). New York: McGraw-Hill, p. viii.

Fiedler, K. (1988). Emotional mood, cognitive style, and behavior regulation. In K. Fiedler & J. P. Forgas (Eds.), *Affect cognition and social behavior* (pp. 100–119). Toronto: Hogrefe.

Gage, G. J., Parikh, H., & Marzullo, T. C. (2008). The cingulate cortex does everything. *Biomedical Engineering, 14*(3), 55.

Gall, Fj., & Spurzheim, G. (1810). Anatomie et physiologie du système nerveux en général et du cerveau en particulier. Tome 1. In *Texte revue de critique et de theorie litteraire.*, Paris: F. Schoel.

Ganel, T., Valyear, K. F., Goshen-Gottstein, Y., & Goodale, M. A. (2005). The involvement of the 'fusiform face area' in processing facial expression. *Neuropsychologia, 43*(11), 1645–1654.

Gardner, H. (1983). *Frames of mind* (2nd ed., p. 463). New York: Basic books (first pub 1984).

Gazzaniga, M. S. (1998). Brain and conscious experience. *Advances in Neurology, 77*(6), 181–192. discussion 192–193.

Gazzaniga, M. S. (2005). Forty-five years of split-brain research and still going strong. *Nature Reviews Neuroscience, 6*(8), 653–659.

Gazzaniga, M. S., Ivry, R. B., & Mangun, G. R. (2008). Cognitive neuroscience: The biology of mind (excerpt). In *Cognitive neuroscience the biology of mind* (pp. 148–159). Cambridge, MA: The MIT Press.

Gelenberg, A. J., Wojcik, J. D., Gibson, C. J., & Wurtman, R. J. (1983). Tyrosine for depression. *Journal of Psychiatric Research, 17*(2), 175–180.

Gerson, M. C., Abdul-Waheed, M., & Millard, R. W. (2009). Of fight and flight. *Journal of Nuclear Cardiology Official Publication of the American Society of Nuclear Cardiology, 16*(2), 176–179.

Glimcher, P., W. et al. (2008). *Neuroeconomics: Decision Making and the Brain*, London: Academic Press.

Goldberg, L. R. (1993). The structure of phenotypic personality traits. *The American Psychologist, 48*(1), 26–34.

Goleman, D., Boyatzis, R., & McKee, A. (2001). Primal leadership: The hidden driver of great performance. *Harvard Business Review, 79*(11), 42–51.

Goleman, D., Boytzis, R., & McKee, A. (2002). *Primal leadership: Realizing the power of emotional intelligence*. Boston: Harvard Business Review Press.

Gordon, M. (2003). Roots of empathy. *The Keio Journal of Medicine, 52*(4), 236–243.

Grawe, K. (2006). *Neuropsychotherapy: How the neurosciences inform effective psychotherapy.* Mahwah: Lawrence Erlbaum Associates.

Greenberg, J., & Baron, R. A. (2008). *Behavior in organizations* (9th ed., Vol. 2, no. 4, p. 276). Upper Saddle River: Prentice Hall.

Gross, C. G. (1998). Galen and the squealing pig. *The Neuroscientist, 4*(3), 216.

Grosse Holforth, M., Grawe, K., & Tamcan, Ö. (2004). *Inkongruenzfragebogen: Manual.* Göttingen: Hogrefe.

Grosse Holtforth, M., & Grawe, K. (2000). Fragebogen zur Analyse Motivationaler Schemata (FAMOS). *Zeitschrift für Klinische Psychologie und Psychotherapie, 29*(3), 170–179.

Grosse Holtforth, M., & Grawe, K. (2003). Der Inkongruenzfragebogen (INK). *Zeitschrift für Klinische Psychologie und Psychotherapie, 32*(4), 315–323.

Grosse Holtforth, M., Pincus, A. L., Grawe, K., Mauler, B., & Castonguay, L. G. (2007). When what you want is not what you get: Motivational correlates of interpersonal problems in clinical and nonclinical samples. *Journal of Social and Clinical Psychology, 26*(10), 1095–1119.

Gullowsen, J. (1972). A measure of work group autonomy. In *Job design* (pp. 374–390). Harmondsworth: Penguin Books.

Gurunluoglu, R., Shafighi, M., Gurunluoglu, A., & Cavdar, S. (2011). Giulio Cesare Aranzio (Arantius) (1530-89) in the pageant of anatomy and surgery. *Journal of Medical Biography, 19*(2), 63–69.

Gyurak, A., Hooker, C. I., Miyakawa, A., Verosky, S., Luerssen, A., & Ayduk, O. N. (2011). Individual differences in neural responses to social rejection: the joint effect of self-esteem and attentional control. *Social Cognitive and Affective Neuroscience, 19*(3), 279–280.

Hackmann, J. R., & Suttle, J. L. (1977). *Improving life at work: Behavioral science approaches to organizational change* (p. 128). Santa Monica: Goodyear.

Haidt, J. (2001). The emotional dog and its rational tail: A social intuitionist approach to moral judgment. *Psychological Review, 108*(4), 814–834.

Hardee, J. E., Thompson, J. C., & Puce, A. (2008). The left amygdala knows fear: Laterality in the amygdala response to fearful eyes. *Social Cognitive and Affective Neuroscience, 3*(1), 47–54.

Harlow, H. F. (1958). The nature of love. *The American Psychologist, 13*(2), 673–685.

Harris, T. A. (1973). *I'm ok – you're ok.* New York: First Avon Books.

Hawking, S., & Mlodinow, L. (2010). *The grand design.* New York: Bantam Books.

Heidecker, K.-M. (2006). Trepanation of the skull in classical antiquity. *Wurzburger medizinhistorische Mitteilungen im Auftrage der Wurzburger medizinhistorischen Gesellschaft und in Verbindung mit dem Institut fur Geschichte der Medizin der Universitat Wurzburg, 25,* 113–131.

Hermann, N. (1996). *The whole brain business book.* New York: McGraw-Hill.

Hersey, P., & Blanchard, K. (1993). *Management of organizational behavior* (Vol. 12, no. 2, pp. 45–65). Englewood Cliffs: Prentice-Hall.

Hersey, P., Blanchard, K. H., & Johnson, D. E. (2001). *Management of organizational behaviour: Leading human resources 8th ed.* Upper Saddle River: Prentice Hall.

Herzberg, F. (2003). One more time: How do you motivate employees? 1968. *Harvard Business Review, 81*(1), 87–96.

Hodgkin, A. L., & Huxley, A. F. (1952). A quantitative description of membrane current and its application to conduction and excitation in nerve. *The Journal of Physiology, 117*(4), 500–544.

Hoffman, B. J., Woehr, D. J., Maldagen-Youngjohn, R., & Lyons, B. D. (2011). Great man or great myth? A quantitative review of the relationship between individual differences and leader effectiveness. *Journal of Occupational and Organizational Psychology, 84*(2), 347–381.

Holmes, D. (2011). Mapping the brain: of mice and men. *The Lancet, 10*(8), 684–685.

Hurley, R. F. (2006). The decision to trust. *Harvard Business Review*(9).

Hüther, G. (2006). *Brainwash – Einführung in die Neurobiologie für Pädagogen.* Auditorium Netzwerk: Therapeuten und Lehrer.

Hüther, G. (2009). Wie gehirngerechte Führung funktioniert: Neurobiologie für Manager. *managerSeminare, 130*, 30–34.

Hüther, G. Zukunft wird jetzt gemacht, in *IV. Know-how-Kongress*, 2309.

Hynie, S., & Klenerová, V. (1991). Neurobiology of memory. *LEncephale, 59*(2), 295–303.

Ioannides, A. A. (2009). Magnetoencephalography (MEG). F. Hyder, ed. *Methods In Molecular Biology Clifton NJ, 489*(1), 167–188.

Isaacson, R. L., Smelser, N. J., & Baltes, P. B. (2001). Limbic System. In N. J. Smelser & P. B. Baltes (Eds.), *International encyclopedia of social behavioral sciences* (Vol. 2, pp. 8858–8862). Amsterdam: Elsevier.

Jones, E. G. (2007). Neuroanatomy: Cajal and after Cajal. *Brain Research Reviews, 55*(2), 248–255.

Kahneman, D., & Tversky, A. (1979). Prospect theory: An analysis of decision under risk. *Econometrica, 47*(2), 263–291.

Kandel, E. R. (2006). *In search of memory* (p. 280). New York: W. W. Norton & Company.

Kandel, E. R. (2006a). *In search of memory* (p. 120). New York: W. W Norton & Company.

Kandel, E. R. (2006b). *In search of memory* (p. 187). New York: W. W. Norton & Company.

Kandel, E. R., & Tauc, L. (1965). Mechanism of heterosynaptic facilitation in the giant cell of the abdominal ganglion of Aplysia depilans. *The Journal of Physiology, 181*(1), 28–47.

Kandel, E. R., Schwartz, J. H., & Jessell, T. M. (2000). *Principles of neural science* (Vol. 3, no. 22, p. 1414). New York: McGraw-Hill.

Kantor, D. B., & Kolodkin, A. L. (2003). Curbing the excesses of youth: Molecular insights into axonal pruning. *Neuron, 38*(6), 849–852.

Kilcross, S. (2000). The amygdala, emotion and learning. *The Psychologist, 13*(10), 502–508.

Kobayashi, M., & Pascual-Leone, A. (2003). Transcranial magnetic stimulation in neurology. *Lancet Neurology, 2*(3), 145–156.

Kolb, B., & Whishaw, I. Q. (1998). Brain plasticity and behavior. *Annual Review of Psychology, 49*(1), 43–64.

Korsten, N., Fragopanagos, N., Taylor, J. G. (2007). *Neural substructures for appraisal in emotion: Self-esteem and depression.* Proceedings of the 17th international conference on artificial neural networks, pp. 850–858.

Kosfeld, M., Heinrichs, M., Zak, P. J., Fischbacher, U., & Fehr, E. (2005). Oxytocin increases trust in humans. *Nature, 435*(7042), 673–676.

Kosfeld, M. et al., 2005. Oxytocin increases trust in humans. *Nature, 435*(7042), pp. 673–676.

Krämer, K., & Nolting, H. D. (2009). *Gesundheitsreport 2009, Analyse der Arbeitsunfähigkeitsdaten: Schwerpunktthema Doping am Arbeitsplatz.* Hamburg: DAK.

Kringelbach, M. L., & Berridge, K. C. (2009). Towards a functional neuroanatomy of pleasure and happiness. *Trends in Cognitive Sciences, 13*(11), 479–487.

Kumari, V., et al. (2004). Personality predicts brain responses to cognitive demands. *The Journal of Neuroscience, 24*, 10636–10641.

Küpers, W., & Weibler, J. (2005). *Emotionen in organisationen.* Stuttgart: Kohlhammer.

Lerch, J., Lau, C., Ng, L., Hawrylycz, M., & Henkelman, R. (2009). The Allen Institute mouse brain gene expression data co-aligned with a mouse MRI atlas. In Proceedings 17th scientific meeting, international society for magnetic resonance in medicine, (Vol. 42, p. 949).

LeDoux, J. E. (1991). Emotion and the limbic system concept. *Concepts in Neuroscience, 2*(2), 169–199.

Lieberman, S. (1956). The effects of changes in roles on the attitudes of role occupants. *Human Relations, 9*(4), 385–402.

Liu, Y. (2003). Nucleus accumbens oxytocin and dopamine interact to regulate pair bond formation in female prairie voles. *Neuroscience, 121*(3), 537–544.

Loukas, M., et al. (2011). Korbinian Brodmann (1868–1918) and his contributions to mapping the cerebral cortex. *Neurosurgery, 68*(1), 6–11; discussion 11. http://www.ncbi.nlm.nih.gov/pubmed/21099724.

MacLean, P. D. (1990). *The triune brain in evolution: Role in paleocerebral functions.* New York: Springer.

Maguire, E. A., Woollett, K., & Spiers, H. J. (2006). London taxi drivers and bus drivers: a structural MRI and neuropsychological analysis. *Hippocampus, 16*(12), 1091–1101.

Maguire, E. A., et al. (2000). Navigation-related structural change in the hippocampi of taxi drivers. *Proceedings of the National Academy of Sciences of the United States of America, 97*(8), 4398–4403.

Mann, D. (2010). Brain-training games won't boost your IQ. *WebMD.* http://www.webmd.com/ brain/news/20100420/brain-training-games-wont-boost-your-iq?print=true.

Manz, C. C., Shipper, F., & Stewart, G. L. (2009). Everyone a team leader: Shared influence at W. L. Gore & Associates. *Organizational Dynamics, 38*(3), 239–244.

Maslow, A. H. (1943). A theory of human motivation. *Psychological Review, 50*(4), 1–21.

Matthews, P., & Jezzard, P. (2004). Functional magnetic resonance imaging. *Journal of Neurology, Neurosurgery & Psychiatry, 82*(4), 6–12.

Matthiesen, A. S., Ransjö-Arvidson, A. B., Nissen, E., & Uvnäs-Moberg, K. (2001). Postpartum maternal oxytocin release by newborns: effects of infant hand massage and sucking. *Birth Berkeley Calif, 28*(1), 13–19.

Mayo, E. (1949). Hawthorne and the western electric company. In D. S. Pugh (Ed.), *Organization theory selected readings.* London: Penguin Books.

McGilchrist, I. (2009). *The master and his emissary: The divided brain and the making of the Western world.* New Haven: Yale University Press.

McIntyre, C. K., Power, A. E., Roozendaal, B., & McGaugh, J. L. (2003). Role of the basolateral amygdala in memory consolidation. *Progress in Neurobiology, 70*(5), 273–293.

Meg, M. (2004). Introduction to magnetoencephalography. *Neurosurgery,* (1), 1–7.

Miller, E. K., & Cohen, J. D. (2001). An integrative theory of prefrontal cortex function. *Annual Review of Neuroscience, 24*(1), 167–202.

Mohr, R. D., & Zoghi, C. (2006). Is job enrichment really enriching? (pp. 76–84). Available at: http//www.bls.gov/ore/pdf/ec060010.pdf.

Murray, E. A. (2007). The amygdala, reward and emotion. *Trends in Cognitive Sciences, 11*(11), 489–497.

Myers, I. (1962). *Myers-Briggs type indicator.* Consulting Psychologists Press.

Nakatani, Y., et al. (2009). Why the carrot is more effective than the stick: different dynamics of punishment memory and reward memory and its possible biological basis. *Neurobiology of Learning and Memory, 92*(3), 370–380.

Neuberger, O. (2006). *Mikropolitik und moral in organisationen.* Stuttgart: UTB GmbH.

Nieoullon, A. (2002). Dopamine and the regulation of cognition and attention. *Progress in Neurobiology, 67*(1), 53–83.

Nishimoto, S., Vu, A. T., Naselaris, T., Benjamini, Y., Yu, B., & Gallant, J. L. (2011). Reconstructing visual experiences from brain activity evoked by natural movies. *Current Biology, 21*(19), 1–6.

Northouse, P. G. (2008). *Introduction to leadership: Concepts and practice* (p. 20). Thousand Oaks: Sage Publications.

Ochsner, K. N., & Gross, J. J. (2005). The cognitive control of emotion. *Trends in Cognitive Sciences, 9*(5), 242–249.

Olds, J., & Milner, P. (1954). Positive reinforcement produced by electrical stimulation of septal area and other areas of the brain. *Journal of Comparative and Physiological Psychology, 47*, 419–427.

Olfert, K. (2010). *Personalwirtschaft* (14th ed.). Ludwigshafen: Kiehl.

Owen, A. M., et al. (2010). Putting Brain Training to the Test. *Nature, 465*(7299), 1–5.

Palmer, L. F. (2002). Bonding matters: The chemistry of attachment. *Attachment Parenting International News, 5*(2), 1–4.

Pascalis, O., et al. (2005). Plasticity of face processing in infancy. *Proceedings of the National Academy of Sciences of the United States of America, 102*(14), 5297–5300.

Perry, E., Walker, M., Grace, J., & Perry, R. (1999). Acetylcholine in mind. *Trends in Neurosciences, 22,* 273–280.

Persky, J. (1995). Retrospectives the ethology of homo economicus. *The Journal of Economic Perspectives, 9*(2), 221–231.

Petrides, M. (2000). The role of the mid-dorsolateral prefrontal cortex in working memory. *Experimental Brain Research Experimentelle Hirnforschung Experimentation Cerebrale, 133*(1), 44–54. Available at: http://www.ncbi.nlm.nih.gov/pubmed/10933209.

Pfeiffer, W., Dörrie, U., & Stoll, E. (1977). *Menschliche Arbeit in der industriellen Produktion.* Göttingen: Vandenhoeck & Ruprecht.

Pillay, S. S. (2009). The neuroscience of change and transformation. New York.

Pillay, S. S. (2010). *Life unlocked.* New York: Rodale Books.

Pillay, S. S. (2011). *Your brain and business.* New Jersey: FT Press.

Ploog, D. (1980). Emotions as products of the limbic system. *Medizinische Psychologie, 6,* 7–19.

Rae, C., Digney, A. L., McEwan, S. R., & Bates, T. C. (2003). Oral creatine monohydrate supplementation improves brain performance: a double-blind, placebo-controlled, cross-over trial. *Proceedings. Biological sciences / The Royal Society, 270*(1529), 2147–2150.

Ramachandran, V. S. (2000). *Mirror neurons and imitation learning as the driving force behind "the great leap forward" in human evolution.* New York: Morrow. http://www.edge.org/3rd_culture/ramachandran/ramachandran_index.html.

Ramachandran, V. (2009). Versus ramachandran: The neurons that shaped civilization. *TEDcom.* http://www.ted.com/talks/vs_ramachandran_the_neurons_that_shaped_civilization.html.

Reif, W. E., & Schoderbek, P. P. (1966). Job enlargement: Antidote to apathy. *Human Resource Management, 5*(1), 16–23.

Rizzolatti, G. (2008). *Mirrors in the brain: How our minds share actions and emotions.* Oxford: Oxford University Press.

Rizzolatti, G., & Fabbri-Destro, M. (2010). Mirror neuron mechanism. In G. F. Koob, M. L. Moal, & R. F. Thompson (Eds.), *Encyclopedia of behavioral neuroscience* (pp. 240–249). Burlington: Academic.

Rizzolatti, G., Fadiga, L., Gallese, V., & Fogassi, L. (1996). Premotor cortex and the recognition of motor actions. *Brain Research, 3*(2), 131–141.

Rock, D. (2008). SCARF: a brain-based model for collaborating with and influencing others SCARF: A brain-based model for collaborating with and influencing others. *NeuroLeadership Journal, 1*(1), 1–9.

Rock, D. (2009). Managing with the brain in mind. *Neuroscience Research, 1*(1), 1.

Rolls, E. T. (2001). Emotion, neural basis of. In N. J. Smelser & P. B. Baltes (Eds.), *International encyclopedia of social behavioral sciences* (pp. 4444–4449). Oxford: Pergamon.

Ross, C. E. (2011). Collective threat, trust, and the sense of personal control. *Journal of Health and Social Behavior, 38*(3), 275–297.

Roth, W. (1999). *The roots and future of management theory: A systems perspective* (pp. 141–145). Boca Raton: CRC Press.

Sacks, O. (1985). *The man who mistook his wife for a hat and other clinical tales (1985).* London: Gerald Duckworth & Co. Ltd.

Sahakian, B., & Morein-Zamir, S. (2007). Professor's little helper. *Nature, 450*(7173), 1157–1159.

Salamon, S. D., & Robinson, S. L. (2008). Trust that binds: The impact of collective felt trust on organizational performance. *Journal of Applied Psychology, 93*(3), 593–601.

Saulsman, L. (2004). The five-factor model and personality disorder empirical literature: A meta-analytic review. *Clinical Psychology Review, 23*(8), 1055–1085.

Saunders, B. T., & Richard, J. M. (2011). Shedding light on the role of ventral tegmental area dopamine in reward. *The Journal of Neuroscience, 31*(50), 18195–18197.

Schacter, D. L. (1996). *Searching for memory: The brain, the mind, and the past.* New York: Basic Books.

Schein, E. H. (1980). *Organizational psychology* (3rd ed.). Eaglewood Cliffs: Prentice-Hall.

Schönpflug, W. (2000). Geschichte der Emotionskonzepte. In J. H. Otto, H. A. Euler, & H. Mandl (Eds.), *Emotionspsychologie Ein Handbuch* (pp. 19–28). Weinheim: Beltz.

Schultz, D., & Schultz, S. E. (2009). *Psychology and work today* (10th ed., pp. 136–144). Upper Saddle River: Prentice Hall.

Seidel, W. (2004). *Emotionale Kompetenz – Gehirnforschung und Lebenskunst.* Heidelberg: Springer.

Selmer, R. (1989). Managing without managers. *Harvard Business Review*, 67(5), 76–84.

Semler, R. (1994). Why my former employees still work for me. *Harvard Business Review*, 72(1), 64–71.

Semler, R. (2006). Out of this world: Doing things the Semco way. In R. P. Gandossy, E. Tucker, & N. Verma (Eds.), *Workforce wake-up call: Your workforce is changing, are you?* (pp. 187–199). Hewitt Associates: Hoboken.

Senge, P. M. (2004). *The fifth discipline: The art and practice of the learning organization* (Vol. 58, no. 2, p. 445). New York: Currency Doubleday.

Setlow, B. (1997). Mini-review the nucleus accumbens and learning and memory. *Journal of Neuroscience Research, 521, no. June*, 515–521.

Sharot, T., Riccardi, A. M., Raio, C. M., & Phelps, E. A. (2007). Neural mechanisms mediating optimism bias. *Nature, 450*(7166), 1–5.

Shaw, C. A., & McEachern, J. C. (2001). *Toward a theory of neuroplasticity.* Philadelphia: Psychology Press.

Shelton, J. T., Elliott, E. M., Matthews, R. A., Hill, B. D., & Gouvier, W. D. (2010). The relationships of working memory, secondary memory, and general fluid intelligence: working memory is special. *Journal of Experimental Psychology: Learning, Memory, and Cognition, 36*(3), 813–820.

Shevel, A. (2007). Out of this world: Doing things the Semco Way. *Business*, 13–21.

Smith, A. (1904). *An inquiry into the nature and causes of the wealth of nations* (5th ed.). London: Methuen & Co., Ltd.. Available at: http://www.econlib.org/library/Smith/smWNCover.html.

Somerville, L. H., Kelley, W. M., & Heatherton, T. F. (2010). Self-esteem modulates medial prefrontal cortical responses to evaluative social feedback. *Cerebral Cortex, 20*(12), 3005–3013.

Sperry, R. W. (1961). Cerebral Organization and Behavior: The split brain behaves in many respects like two separate brains, providing new research possibilities. *Science, 133*(3466), 1749–1757.

Spillane, R. (2012). Why workplaces must resist the cult of personality testing. Available at: http://theconversation.edu.au/why-workplaces-must-resist-the-cult-of-personality-testing-5540 [Accessed 12 September 2012].

Squire, L. R. (2009). The legacy of patient H.M. for neuroscience. *Neuron, 61*(1), 6–9.

Sternberg, R. J. (2008). Increasing fluid intelligence is possible after all. *Proceedings of the National Academy of Sciences of the United States of America, 105*(19), 6791–6792.

Storch, M. (2004). Resource-activating Selfmanagement with the Zurich Resource Model (ZRM). *European Psychotherapy, 5*(1), 27–64.

Swaab, D. F., Bao, A.-M., & Lucassen, P. J. (2005). The stress system in the human brain in depression and neurodegeneration. *Ageing Research Reviews, 4*(2), 141–194.

Talbot, M. (2009). Brain gain: The underground world of neuroenhancing drugs. *New Yorker New York NY 1925*, 32–43.

Taylor, F. W, (1911). *Principles of Scientific Management.* New York: Harper & Brothers.

Thompson, L., Thompson, M., & Reid, A. (2010). Neurofeedback Outcomes in Clients with Asperger's Syndrome. *Applied Psychophysiology and Biofeedback, 35*(1), 63–81.

Tixier-Vidal, A. (2010). From the cell theory to the neuron theory. *Biologie aujourdhui, 204*(4), 253–266.

Tournier, J.-D., Mori, S., & Leemans, A. (2011). Diffusion tensor imaging. *Rinsho shinkeigaku Clinical neurology, 48*(6), 1532–1556.

Trimble, M. (2011). The master and his emissary: The divided brain and the making of the western world. *Cognitive Neuropsychiatry, 16*(3), 125–128.

Tupes, E. C., & Christal, R. E. (1961). *Recurrent personality factors based on trait raitings (Technical report ASD-TR-61-97).* Wiley Online Library.

Turner, L., & Sandberg, A. (1996). Enriching production. Perspectives on Volvo's Uddevalla plant as an alternative to lean production – Sandberg, A. *mpraubunimuenchende, 50*(2), 359.

Ulich, E. (2005). *Arbeitspsychologie.* Stuttgart: Schäffer-Poeschel.

Van Den Bos, W., et al. (2009). What motivates repayment? Neural correlates of reciprocity in the Trust Game. *Social Cognitive and Affective Neuroscience, 4*(3), 294–304.

Van Maurik, J. (2001). *Writers on leadership.* London: Penguin.

Van Winkle, E. (2000). The toxic mind: The biology of mental illness and violence. *Medical Hypotheses, 55*(1), 356–368.

Vanderburg, D. (2004). The story of Semco: The company that humanized work. *Bulletin of Science Technology Society, 24*(5), 430–434.

Vroom, V. H., & Yetton, P. W. (1973). *Leadership and decision-making* (Vol. 18, no. 4, p. 556). Pittsburgh: University of Pittsburgh Press.

Watt, D. F. (1999). Towards a science of consciousness III: The third Tucson discussion and debates. In S. R. Hameroff, A. W. Kazniak, & D. J. Chalmers (Eds.), At the intersection of emotion and consciousness: Affective neuroscience and extended reticular thalamic activating system (ERTAS) theories of consciousness (p. 216). Cambridge, MA: MIT Press.

Whalen, P. J. (1998). Fear, vigilance, and ambiguity: Initial neuroimaging studies of the human amygdala. *Current Directions in Psychological Science, 7*(6), 177–188.

Whalen, P. J., Rauch, S. L., Etcoff, N. L., McInerney, S. C., Lee, M. B., & Jenike, M. A. (1998). Masked presentations of emotional facial expressions modulate amygdala activity without explicit knowledge. *The Journal of Neuroscience, 18*(1), 411–418.

Whalen, P. J., Shin, L. M., McInerney, S. C., Fischer, H., Wright, C. I., & Rauch, S. L. (2001). A functional MRI study of human amygdala responses to facial expressions of fear versus anger. *Emotion Washington Dc, 1*(1), 70–83.

Whitmore, J. (2002). *Coaching for performance* (3rd ed.). London: Nicholas Brealey.

Williams, L. M. (2006). An integrative neuroscience model of 'significance' processing. *Journal of Integrative Neuroscience, 5*(1), 1–47.

Williams, M. (2007). Building genuine trust through interpersonal emotion management: A threat regulation model of trust and collaboration across boundaries. *The Academy of Management Review, 32*(2), 595–621.

Williams, J. H., Whiten, A., Suddendorf, T., & Perrett, D. I. (2001). Imitation, mirror neurons and autism. *Neuroscience and Biobehavioral Reviews, 25*(4), 287–295.

Wise, R. A. (2002). Brain reward circuitry. *Neuron, 36*, 229–240.

Zak, P. J., (2004). Neuroeconomics. *Philosophical Transactions of the Royal Society of London. Series B, Biological Sciences, 359*(1451), 1737–1748.

Zink, C. F., Tong, Y., Chen, Q., Bassett, D. S., Stein, J. L., & Meyer-Lindenberg, A. (2008). Know your place: Neural processing of social hierarchy in humans. *Neuron, 58*(2), 273–283.

Index

A. Ghadiri et al., *Neuroleadership*, Management for Professionals,
DOI 10.1007/978-3-642-30165-0, © Springer-Verlag Berlin Heidelberg 2012

CPSIA information can be obtained at www.ICGtesting.com
Printed in the USA
LVOW01*0757140713

342771LV00012B/623/P